Tracing Your Civil War Ancestor

Tracing Your Civil War Ancestor/ *BY*

BERTRAM HAWTHORNE GROENE

JOHN F. BLAIR, *Publisher*
Winston-Salem, N. C.

Second Printing, 1977

COPYRIGHT © 1973 BY
JOHN F. BLAIR, PUBLISHER
LIBRARY OF CONGRESS CATALOG
CARD NUMBER: 73–77903
ALL RIGHTS RESERVED
ISBN 0–89587–000–2
PRINTED IN THE UNITED STATES
OF AMERICA BY
WINSTON PRINTING COMPANY
WINSTON-SALEM, N.C.

For My Parents /

CHARLES BERTRAM AND
LUCILLE HAWTHORNE GROENE

Acknowledgments

In creating a guidebook such as this, an author very soon finds himself indebted to many people. I will list here only a few: James Walker of the National Archives; Charles E. Dornbusch, eminent Civil War bibliographer; Bill Moore of Baton Rouge, noted collector and expert on Civil War arms; Robert Reilly, authority on United States military weapons; Dr. J. Larry Crain, martial arms expert, genealogist, and assistant secretary for Louisiana's Department of Culture, Recreation and Tourism; and Bill R. Linder, director of the Central Reference Division of the National Archives. All these persons were a source of aid and comfort by giving help, advice, and encouragement.

The author also wishes to express his appreciation to the following publishers and others who graciously gave their consent for the use of illustrative material and helped in various ways:

To the Louisiana State University Press for permission to reproduce a page from *Civil War Books,* by Allan Nevins, James I. Robertson, Jr., and Bell I. Wiley.

To the New York Public Library for permission to reproduce two pages from Volume II of *Military Bibliography of the Civil War,* by Charles E. Dornbusch.

To A. S. Barnes & Company, Inc., for permission to reproduce a page from its edition of *A Compendium of the War of the Rebellion,* by Frederick H. Dyer.

To the University of Illinois Press for permission to reproduce a page from its edition of *Historical Register and Dictionary of the United States Army,* by Francis B. Heitman.

To the Yale University Press for permission to reproduce a page from *A Guide to Archives and Manuscripts in the United States,* edited by Philip M. Hamer.

To Robert M. Reilly for permission to reproduce a page from his book, *United States Military Small Arms, 1816–1865,* published by The Eagle Press, Inc., Baton Rouge, Louisiana, and also for permission to raid his bibliography for material for my Appendix D.

To the Library of Congress for invaluable assistance.

To the National Archives for permission to reproduce a number of records.

Last, I am indebted to my wife Peggy, who typed, edited, and helped revise this book many times since its inception.

Contents

Illustrations

Introduction

This book has been especially designed as a guide for those who are descendants of Civil War veterans. It should also be highly useful to collectors of Civil War equipment and to antique dealers.

Descendants of Civil War veterans can use this book to help trace the military careers of their forebears, to follow their battles and camp experiences, and to study in depth the histories of their military and naval units. With luck, the book may even lead to a photograph of great-grandfather or his comrades and officers.

Collectors of Civil War items can use this guide to trace names inscribed on weapons and other military equipment, thus regaining for such items a lost time and place in history.

Antique dealers should find the book useful in that it not only aids in establishing a history for inscribed photographs, weapons, and other items, but directs them to the most authoritative sources when they are searching for the identification of Civil War equipment. With its help, they should be able to answer such questions as "Is this truly of the Civil War period?" and even "What is it?"

Tracing Your
Civil War
Ancestor

Scabbard of the sword carried by the officer who stopped the Confederate fleet in the last fight between ironclads in the Civil War. A complete inscription such as this makes a search much easier.

1 / The Value of a Search

On the table in front of me as I write lies a Civil War officer's sword. It has a bright brass guard, and the handle is wrapped, as they were in those days, with sharkskin bound with neatly twisted brass wire. Inscribed on the brass top of the metal scabbard is

Presented to
LT. E. P. MASON
1st Conn Artillery
by his friends in
New Haven

On May 11, 1861, one month after the Civil War began, strapping, nineteen-year-old, six-foot Ebenezer Mason of Litchfield, Connecticut, walked into a Hartford recruiting station. Here he enlisted as a private in the Fourth Connecticut Infantry. Seven months later the Fourth Connecticut was changed to the First Connecticut Heavy Artillery, and now Mason found himself an artillery corporal. In the following months Mason and his comrades hauled their huge mortars and giant rifled cannon into battle after battle as the Union army under McClellan pressed on toward the Rebel capital of Richmond. In December, 1862, Ebenezer was promoted to second lieutenant and was in the bloody tragedies of Fredericksburg, Chancellorsville, and Gettysburg. Mason lived through these battles to become a first lieutenant commanding his own fort, Battery Sawyer, perched on the high south bank of the James River some twelve miles southeast of the Confederate capital. This was an important position, for it protected a water barrier of boats, nets, and masts which the Union army had thrown up across the river. This barrier had been built to prevent a large Confederate fleet trapped up the James River near Richmond from suddenly steaming down the river, anchoring off City Point, Grant's supply base, and shelling that huge depot to a smoking ruin. On the night of

January 23, 1865, an eleven-ship fleet headed by three giant Confederate ironclads, *Fredericksburg, Richmond,* and *Virginia,* attempted just that. Lieutenant Mason's two huge seacoast mortars, which could toss hundred-pound balls a mile into the air, and one large cannon, which could throw a hundred-pound shell over two thousand yards, went into action. They filled the dark, winding river below them with thousands upon thousands of pounds of shells, grapeshot, and canister. Up the river from City Point came the Federal ironclad, *Conestoga,* and because of its fire, that of two other small forts, and Lieutenant Mason's constant battering, the ships of the Confederate fleet were forced to turn their prows west and steam, crippled and defeated, back up the river toward the capital. So ended the last battle with ironclads in the Civil War. Mason's bravery and cool judgment under fire earned him the two bars of a captain of artillery.

Two months later the fatigue, exposure, and strain of more than three years of constant battle took their final toll, and Captain Mason—whether violently or quietly we shall never know—slipped into insanity and was discharged from the army. Throughout the rest of his life Ebenezer Mason was in and out of mental institutions, finally dying childless, divorced, and bitter, in 1911, at the age of sixty-nine.

Captain Mason's story was not a difficult one to trace, and you should be able to do the same with your own soldier's story, with a little time and at very little expense, by following the suggestions in this book.

The ever-growing number of descendants of Johnny Reb and Billy Yank can be divided into several categories. There are those who honestly admit that they know little or absolutely nothing about great-grandfather's war experiences. Most descendants fall into this category. There are those, innocent and pure of heart, who have had handed down to them, intact and without benefit of research, a complete history. A hundred years of time, the faded memories of the old folk, and a few tall tales thrown in that grow more grand with each retelling take their toll. What finally emerges as great-grandfather's history may well resemble the script of a Hollywood historical extravaganza and contain just about as much truth. Then there are those few who really have a complete account of their ancestor passed to them through letters and diaries, but here and there great-grandfather may have stretched a point or two for the "folks back home."

In any case, after reading this book, perhaps you will be one of those brave few who will "go a-searching" on the trail of your forebears and will place your trust in the records whenever you can. You will have tried to find the truth about a noble ancestor. What better tribute could one pay to those who fought in that far-off war than to retrace their steps, buried and forgotten for three generations?

The knowledge of historical research that this book gives will, I hope, provide a history to those who have none, correct fanciful and erroneous histories and replace them with fact, and finally, give additional details to incomplete lives already partially researched by proud and concerned descendants.

Unknown to most people, there are millions of impersonal state and federal records and thousands of books that have preserved literally hundreds of thousands of soldiers' lives and wartime experiences. To those with the know-how of Civil War research they will open the door and unlock the past. An identifying name and regiment can lift any long-dead soldier's personal equipment out of the great flood of existing guns, swords, knives, boots, spurs, or whatever and give it a distinct identity, a place in time, and above all, an authentic history.

On the following two pages is the report of Lieutenant E. P. Mason found in the 128-volume set, Official Record of the Union and Confederate Armies in the War of the Rebellion. *In Mason's own words he tells how he directed the cannon fire that helped turn back the attacking Rebel fleet on the James River in January, 1865. Such a report by one of your ancestors may also be in these volumes.*

mortars on Cemetery Hill battery, which was firing on our troops in rear of Fort Haskell. The other mortars were directed on the batteries near the Petersburg pike. They burst a large number of shell in the fort, wounding four men of the Fifty-first Pennsylvania; no casualties in Company A. They opened one new mortar where they were digging day before yesterday, in rear of the Crater.

Very respectfully, your obedient servant,
H. D. PATTERSON,
Lieutenant, First Connecticut Artillery, Commanding Battery.

Lieut. W. S. MALONY,
Acting Assistant Adjutant-General, Siege Batteries.

No. 16.

Report of Lieut. Ebenezer P. Mason, First Connecticut Heavy Artillery, commanding Battery Sawyer, of operations January 23–24.

BATTERY SAWYER,
James River, Va., January 29, 1865.

SIR: Pursuant to instructions from headquarters Siege Artillery, Line of Bermuda Hundred, dated January 28, 1865, I have the honor to submit the following report of the part taken by this battery in the engagement with the rebel rams on the 23d and 24th instant:

About 8 p. m. the 23d Fort Brady opened fire; the Cox Ferry batteries replied; I opened, hoping to draw the enemy's fire from Fort Brady, in order to enable Captain Pierce to serve his guns more rapidly on the rebel rams, if they were in the river. I was partially successful, drawing the fire of two 10-inch columbiads and one 8-inch rifled gun. I expended five case-shot, six percussion-shell, 100-pounder, and five 10-inch mortar shell.

At 10 p. m. Lieutenant Reed, commanding navy picket detachment, reported to me that a high-pressure side wheel steamer lay at the obstructions and was attempting to remove them, and that two rams lay in the channel about 400 yards above. The night was so dark that I was unable to discover their exact positions excepting by the explosion of the shell from Battery Parsons. I fired at the rams three 100-pounder solid shot, at intervals of about fifteen minutes, with what effect I am unable to tell, and at the steamer nine 10-inch mortar shell, nearly all of which burst well, annoying the men at work on the obstructions very much. At 12.30 a. m. the rams dropped down the river to the obstructions where my 100-pounder would not bear on them. At 3 a. m. the 24th one ram dropped down the stream opposite Sleepy Hollow, about 550 yards from the battery, and remained there at anchor about forty-five minutes. While she lay there one mortar shell, fired at 60 degrees elevation, charge twelve ounces, without bursting charge, struck her on the deck without any visible effect; immediately after, however, she hove up her anchor and changed her position. Thinking it might be her intention to land a force of marines and attack the battery and destroy the signal tower, I posted the supernumerary men (about thirty), with muskets, near the wharf, to prevent any boats landing. The ram, after dropping down stream about 100 yards, changed her course and steamed up the river out of sight; not being able to discover her position I ceased firing until daylight. While she lay opposite Sleepy Hollow I fired at her nineteen mortar shell, at 60 degrees elevation, without bursting charge; I cannot state positively that but one struck her. The firing was very accurate, all the shell striking within a radius of ten yards. Soon after daylight I discovered the rams in the channel, about 2,000 yards distant, and partially covered by the bank of the river and a grove of trees. I again opened and fired from the 100-pounder six case-shot, three percussion, and twelve solid shot, and from the mortars thirty-one shell; four solid shot, one percussion, two case-shot, and two mortar shells struck the rams. From this point the only visible damage was by the case-shot, which perforated the smoke-stacks; the percussion-shell burst against her side. The solid shot did not appear to penetrate—some of them after striking rolled back into the water, others ricochetted beyond.

I also fired after daylight at the land batteries (not being able to bear on the rams), with the 100-pounder, eleven case-shot. At about 12 m. the rams succeeded in getting off the bar and steamed around the bend. During the morning of the 24th the battery received the fire of three 10-inch columbiads, one 8-inch and one 7-inch rifled gun.

No casualties occurred.

The men behaved with the utmost coolness and served the pieces with skill and alacrity.

I am, very respectfully, your obedient servant,

E. P. MASON,
First Lieut., First Regiment Connecticut Arty., Comdg. Battery.
Lieut. CHARLES A. TRUESDELL,
Adjutant First Connecticut Artillery.

No. 17.

Report of Lieut. John O'Brien, First Connecticut Heavy Artillery, commanding Battery No. 4, of operations March 25.

BATTERY NO. 4,
Before Petersburg, Va., March 26, 1865.

LIEUTENANT: I have the honor to submit the following report of the part sustained by Company I, First Connecticut Artillery, the garrison of Battery No. 4, during the engagement of yesterday:

At 4 o'clock in the morning I heard firing on the line near Battery No. 10, but I supposed it was wholly confined to the pickets. At 5.30, an hour and a half later, I saw indications that an advance had been made by the enemy upon our lines near Battery No. 10. I had the company under arms and made arrangements for a defense, when I received orders to open on the enemy, who were now in possession of Fort Stedman and Battery No. 10; these orders were received at daylight. I fired 130 rounds of percussion and 6 rounds of time-fuse shell, nearly all of which were thrown into an advancing column of the enemy, which was in rear of the last-named work. About fifteen shell were thrown into the Chesterfield battery. This battery opened upon Battery No. 5 and the line of works near it, and six shell were thrown into a retreating column of the enemy when it was on the plain in front of Battery No. 9. Fearing an advance, in case of the failure of a pending charge by our forces, fired only when the enemy's troops were in sight, having only about 100 rounds for each piece (three pieces).

I am, sir, very respectfully, your obedient servant,

JOHN O'BRIEN,
First Lieut., First Connecticut Artillery, Comdg. Battery No. 4.
Lieut. W. S. MALONY,
A. A. A. G., Siege Batteries, Before Petersburg, Va.

On the practical side, a name and regiment increases the cash value of an antique. A traceable soldier's name on a revolver will add at least one-third to its value and will easily double the price of a sword, whether enlisted man's or officer's. As an example, I recently purchased two swords from a large antique weapons dealer in the East. The sword with the name of the owner, Captain Robert P. Barry, cost about $100. An almost identical sword, but with no name or other identifying mark, cost around $50. These prices are now out of date, but the large price gap between the identifiable and the unknown will remain the same and in all probability will widen in the years to come.

A knowledge of the techniques of Civil War research may be the only way you can acquire a truly fine antique at a bargain-basement price. Suppose, in an antique shop, you have found a Union officer's sword with a name inscribed on the hilt. Now, neither you nor the dealer has ever heard of the man. With a basic knowledge of how to search out a name, you can, within a few hours or at the very most within one or two weeks, come up with an answer as to who the man was. The fact may be that this unknown man entered the war as a lieutenant but finished as a general. He may never have risen above the rank of lieutenant but may have lived and died a hero's death with that sword in his hand, or he may have been an aide to General Grant or General Sherman. Then again, he may have been a shabby traitor, as the original owner of a sword of a friend once proved to be, or perhaps he was a nobody with a record of practically no interest. He may even be a fictitious character whose name was inscribed on a weapon simply to defraud a buyer. The possibilities are endless, but in any case, you will want to know.

Not long ago, at one of those small-town antique shows where you expect to find nothing, I saw an inconspicuous Colt cap-and-ball six-shooter sticking out of a timeworn holster. There was nothing unusual about it except an inscription engraved on the brass backstrap of the gun, "Francis Preston Blair, Jr.," in beautiful script and under that in bold block letters "St. Louis

Two nearly identical Union officers' swords. The sword inscribed "Capt. Robert P. Barry" was found to have a traceable history so is worth at least twice as much as the uninscribed weapon. Its history was a bit hard to trace because of the scant inscription. Here Heit-man's Historical Register and Dictionary of the United States Army *came in very handy. See page 59.*

Above is Francis Preston Blair, Jr., Major General commanding the Fifteenth and Seventeenth Corps under Sherman, friend of Lincoln, senator and congressman from Missouri, and the Democratic nominee for Vice-President of the United States in 1868. Courtesy of the Library of Congress.

Below is his Colt revolver that went unnoticed and unsold on a dealer's table until it was identified and bought by a collector who knew how to trace the name on the backstrap.

Mo." The owner of the gun did not know who Blair was. As a historian, I knew that Francis Preston Blair was a famous politician and close friend of Andrew Jackson. The "Jr.," however, failed to ring a bell. A quick twenty-minute trip home and there was Francis Preston Blair, Jr., listed, with photographs, in every major reference book on my library shelf. Fortified with these facts and figures, I bought the gun.

Blair is one of Missouri's most famous men. A close friend of Lincoln, and both a United States representative and a senator, he was the political leader responsible for holding Missouri in the Union. He served as a major general of the Fifteenth and Seventeenth Corps in Sherman's Army that marched through Georgia, and he ended his long career by being nominated as the Democratic Vice-Presidential candidate in the election of 1868.

With a knowledge of where to look, I was able to buy a priceless antique gun—really a museum piece—for very little. Had the dealer from whom I bought that gun been able to identify the name as I did, you can imagine the profit he could have had. My case was not really unusual. Countless valuable and identifiable antiques exchange hands at low prices or go unnoticed and unsold because of the ignorance of buyers and sellers of, or their indifference to, the fact that names can be traced—and with no great difficulty at that.

As for you hardened collectors of soldiers' gear who, for reasons of time or opportunity or whatever, have never tried to master historical research beyond writing to the National Archives, cheer up! With this book as a starting guide, the next time your neighbor hefts your inscribed Colt .44 Army revolver, comments on its great weight, and says, as you are braced from long experience to hear: "Boy, if that old gun could only talk!" you can take him by the arm, lead him to a comfortable chair, and *make that old gun talk!*

2 / The National Archives

*Thousands upon thousands of beginning research-*ers believe there are no more complete records than those held by the United States Bureau of Archives and Records in Washington, D.C. There is a lot of truth to this. These archives include nearly a million cubic feet of records holding every conceivable type of information, carefully collected and hoarded by the federal government since the founding of our country. The National Archives are open to all, and it is worth a trip to Washington just to be led around and shown what has been preserved for the ages and is at your disposal.

The archives are a vast and priceless source of history. They are doubly important to the occasional researcher because the federal government has a trained professional staff who will search through the millions of records in order to answer your questions. These people will give you more information in answer to your mail request than almost any other source. Just a tiny fraction of the Civil War material available from the National Archives includes

1. Compiled military service records for each soldier, whether volunteer or regular, Union or Confederate
2. Most of the compiled Union and Confederate Naval and Marine Corps service records
3. Union pension records for all state volunteers and regulars, Army, Navy, and Marines
4. Court-martial case file records
5. Medical records on individual soldiers
6. Prisoner of war records
7. Draft records
8. Burial records

The truly staggering amount of military records held by the National Archives can best be appreciated by sending for two of the archives' books. The first is a description of the archives'

Union records by Kenneth W. Munden and Henry P. Beers entitled *Guide to Federal Archives Relating to the Civil War*, 1962, National Archives Publication No. 63–1. In this excellent book the authors describe in detail each kind of record and where it may be found, including personnel records, records for forts and camps, cavalry bureau records, squadron and flotilla records, Marine Corps records, and so on. The Table of Contents lists well over 140 separate bureaus. Six years later Mr. Beers turned out a second volume, this one about the Confederacy, entitled *Guide to the Archives of the Government of the Confederate States of America*, National Archives Publication No. 68–15.

Since the federal government searchers will do a great deal of looking for you, these books are not really necessary for an average search request. But if you want to squeeze every last drop of information from your soldier or regiment, these two books are indispensable. They list the type and location of millions of pages of records held not only by the National Archives but by your own and other states and by museums, colleges, universities, and the like. What a lifesaver they are for professional Civil War historians! To obtain these two books write to

United States Superintendent of Documents
United States Government Printing Office
Washington, D.C. 20402

The archives have also published a 145-page paperback book entitled *Guide to Genealogical Records in the National Archives*, National Archives Publication No. 64–8, by M. B. Colket, Jr., and Frank E. Bridgers. Although not nearly so complete with respect to Civil War references as the Beers and Munden books, it gives a really first-rate idea of how to get the most out of the archives' holdings. Not limited to the Civil War, it begins with the Revolutionary soldier and goes to World War II. It is a truly excellent little book. It also may be ordered from the Superintendent of Documents, using the address given above.

To begin a mail-order search at the national level, you must

supply some information. You must provide the searchers with
the last name of your soldier or sailor, and it is highly desirable
to know his first initial, or better still, his full name. You must
also know his military unit: the First Connecticut Heavy Artillery, Seventh New York Infantry, Twenty-sixth Mississippi Infantry, U.S.S. *Monitor,* C.S.S. *Alabama,* or whatever it may be.
The government archivists will not, for love or money, search for
Private Henry Jones, Ohio Infantry, and they will be reluctant
to look for Private Smith, Twenty-eighth Mississippi, since there
may possibly be fifteen Henry Joneses and two hundred Private
Smiths. Falling short of a complete or partially complete name,
and lacking the soldier's military unit, you must fall back on the
alternatives outlined further on in this book.

Assuming that you have a name and military outfit, your next
step is to address a short letter to

> Military Service Records (NNCC)
> National Archives (GSA)
> Washington, D.C. 20408

Make a brief statement of whom you wish to research and request
five or six sets of order form GSA 6751 so that you may order
photocopies concerning your veteran. This is the form that is
used for researching any veteran from the Revolution to the
Spanish-American War.

In about three weeks to a month you will receive your GSA
6751 forms. This form changes quite often. The present one
has an original white form with three copies beneath it. When
you write heavily with a ball-point pen or type on the original,
the forms underneath become automatic copies. In the first block
of the form you should check that you want both pension and
military records. If you are lucky and they send you both, you
will be charged separately for each.

The present charge is three dollars per record group, but that
will probably increase shortly. If they find nothing, there is no
charge for the search. The three-dollar charge is really a bargain,

since the cost to the government for your search is much more than that. But some agency in that vast bureaucracy of ours pays the difference in a subsidy to the Archives. The directions on the form will tell you to send one GSA 6751 set to the government for each soldier you wish searched.

What may not be quite so clear to the beginning researcher is that the record of a man's military service in any one organization is wholly separate from the record of his service in any other organization. This means that if your ancestor joined the Sixteenth New York and later transferred to the Twenty-eighth, your GSA 6751 request will get you his service in only the one unit you requested, the Sixteenth New York. It will take another GSA 6751 form set to get his service record with the Twenty-eighth New York. You will be billed for each form answered.

Send the forms and see what your inquiry brings. If your soldier was an enlisted volunteer, the chances are that not more than ten pages of records exist. If, however, your soldier was an officer, there is a much better chance that there are extensive records. This is especially true if he was a commanding officer, an inspector, a commissary officer, a regimental adjutant, a surgeon, or perhaps a chaplain. Where officers are concerned, there may be thirty more pages of which you are totally unaware and of which no one will tell you unless you inquire. If you have reason to believe from the rank and position of responsibility of your soldier that there may be more than ten pages, the best approach is to staple a note or write across the top of your GSA form, "Send all military records." Then sit back and wait for from one to three months. If many documents arrive, your bill may be in excess of three dollars, but it is unlikely to be more than ten or twelve dollars, and you will be fortunate if they find enough for the extra charge.

If the military records indicate that great-grandfather was given a general court-martial (a secret the family has successfully hidden for a hundred years or so), reach for another GSA 6751, fill it out, and staple a note or write across the top, "Please send

		Date received by National Archives
ORDER AND BILLING **FOR COPIES OF** **VETERAN'S RECORDS**	*Please read information on the back and follow instructions below.* Submit a separate set of order forms for each veteran. Do not remove any of the sheets of this 4-part set. You will be billed $2.00 for each file reproduced. *Do not mail payment with your order.* This form will be returned to you and serves as your bill when we fill your order.	

Mail the complete set of this order to ▶ Military Service Records (NNCC), National Archives (GSA), Washington, DC 20408

1. CHECK RECORD DESIRED	REQUIRED MINIMUM IDENTIFICATION OF VETERAN		
☐ PENSION ☐ BOUNTY LAND WARRANT APPLICATION *(Service before 1856 only)* ☐ MILITARY	2. VETERAN *(Give last, first and middle names)*		3. STATE FROM WHICH HE SERVED
	4. WAR IN WHICH, OR DATES BETWEEN WHICH HE SERVED	5. IF SERVICE WAS CIVIL WAR ☐ UNION ☐ CONFEDERATE	

PLEASE PROVIDE THE FOLLOWING INFORMATION IF KNOWN

6. UNIT IN WHICH HE SERVED *(Name of regiment or number, company, etc., or name of ship)*	7. BRANCH IN WHICH HE SERVED ☐ INFANTRY ☐ CAVALRY ☐ ARTILLERY ☐ NAVY	*If other, specify:*
	8.. KIND OF SERVICE ☐ VOLUNTEERS ☐ REGULARS	9. PENSION OR BOUNTY LAND FILE NUMBER
10. DATE OF BIRTH	11. PLACE OF BIRTH *(City, county, State, etc.)*	12. NAME OF WIDOW OR OTHER CLAIMANT
13. DATE OF DEATH	14. PLACE OF DEATH	15. IF VETERAN LIVED IN A HOME FOR SOLDIERS, GIVE LOCATION *(City and State)*

16. PLACE(S) VETERAN LIVED AFTER SERVICE

---

17. YOUR NAME AND ADDRESS

City & State / *Number & Street* / *Name* / *Type or print legibly PRESS HARD*

(ZIP code)

DO NOT WRITE BELOW - SPACE IS FOR NATIONAL ARCHIVES TO REPLY TO YOU

☐ **THIS IS YOUR BILL**	RECORDS ENCLOSED ▶ ☐ PENSION ☐ BOUNTY LAND ☐ MILITARY
	NUMBER OF FILES FROM WHICH COPIES WERE REPRODUCED **AMOUNT DUE** ▶ $
	Please remit the above amount in the enclosed addressed envelope with the white copy of this form.

☐ **WE WERE UNABLE TO COMPLETE YOUR ORDER**	RECORDS SEARCHED FOR BUT NOT FOUND ▶ ☐ PENSION ☐ BOUNTY LAND ☐ MILITARY

☐ We found _____ pension or bounty land files and _____ military service files for veterans of the same name (or similar variations). You may order copies by returning the enclosed, marked forms.

☐ When we are unable to find a record for a veteran, this does not necessarily mean that he did not serve. You may be able to obtain information about him from the State archives.

☐ See attached forms/leaflets/information sheet.   ☐ See reverse.

☐ Please *complete* items 2 *(give full name)*, 3 and 4, and resubmit.

SEARCHER	FILE DESIGNATION
DATE	
CASHIER	

18. NUMBER OF BLANK ORDER FORMS YOU WOULD LIKE SENT TO YOU ▶

GENERAL SERVICES ADMINISTRATION   **GSA** FORM **6751** (REV. 2-75)

The front of the white master copy of form GSA 6751 (Rev. 2-75), the form with which you begin all your searches in the National Archives for early veterans.

IMPORTANT INFORMATION

Use this form to order photocopies of records of veterans who served in the United States or Confederate armed forces. These records include:

PENSION APPLICATION FILES based on United States (not State) service before World War I.

> *NOTE: Pensions based on military service for the Confederate States of America were authorized by some Southern States but not by the Federal Government until 1959. Inquiries about State pensions should be addressed to the State archives or equivalent agency at the capital of the veteran's State of residence after the war.*

BOUNTY-LAND WARRANT APPLICATION FILES based on United States (not State) service before 1856.

> *NOTE: Pension or bounty-land warrant application files usually include an official statement of the veteran's military or naval service, as well as information of a personal or genealogical nature. If we find such a file, we send copies of the documents we feel will be most useful to you.*

MILITARY SERVICE RECORDS based on service in the United States Army (officers who served before June 30, 1917, enlisted men before October 31, 1912), Navy (officers and enlisted men who served before 1886), Marine Corps (officers and enlisted men who served before 1896), and Confederate armed forces (1861-65). (We cannot provide photocopies of files for veterans whose service terminated less than 75 years ago, however we are usually able to provide certain information from the files).

> *NOTE: Military service records rarely contain family information. The record of a man's service in any one organization is entirely separate from the record of his service in any other organization. We are ordinarily unable to accurately establish the identity of men of the same name who served in different organizations. If you know that a man served in more than one organization and you desire copies of his military service record, submit a separate form for the service record in each organization.*

DO NOT USE THIS FORM TO REQUEST PHOTOCOPIES OF RECORDS RELATING TO SERVICE IN WORLD WARS I OR II OR SUBSEQUENT SERVICE. WRITE TO: NATIONAL PERSONNEL RECORDS CENTER, GSA, (MILITARY PERSONNEL RECORDS), 9700 PAGE BOULEVARD, ST. LOUIS, MO 63132.

When you send more than one form at a time, each order may be handled separately; you may not receive all your replies at the same time.

When we cite from our indexes that we have numerous files for veterans of the name given, we suggest that you visit the National Archives and examine the various files, or hire a professional researcher to examine each file for you. As a matter of policy the National Archives does not perform research for individuals; we are thus unable to make a file-by-file check to see if the information in the numerous files matches the information you have provided. The Board for Certification of Genealogists, 1307 New Hampshire Avenue, NW., Washington, DC 20036, can provide you with the names of persons in the Washington area willing to do research for a fee. Also, genealogical researchers advertise their services in The Genealogical Helper, the most widely circulated genealogical magazine, available in most libraries having a genealogical section, or by subscription from Everton Publishers, P.O. Box 368, Logan, Utah 84321.

When, because of the size of a file, we are unable to provide copies of all documents, we send copies of the documents we feel will be most useful to you. You may order copies of all documents in a file by making such a specific request and authorizing us to bill you at 15¢ per page ($2 minimum).

More information about the availability of armed service records may be found in our free package of genealogical information leaflets and forms, available by writing to the address on the front of this form.

GSA FORM **6751 BACK** (REV. 2-75)

The reverse side of the National Archives form GSA 6751 (Rev. 2-75) lists important instructions for locating your service man.

all court-martial records." You do this because the military records do not include court-martial records, nor will you be informed of their existence unless you request them. Unfortunately for descendants, Confederate court-martial records are almost nonexistent, so there is little need to bother asking for them.

This is not the end of the use of form GSA 6751. If you either suspect, or the pension or military records show, that your soldier was sick, wounded, or disabled in any way, reach for yet another GSA 6751, fill it out, and staple a note or write across the top, "Please send complete medical records." You must do this because, as in the case of court-martial records, medical records are not included in the military records, and researchers in the archives will not tell you that they exist unless you specifically request them.

It was in just such a way that I uncovered the detailed story of a Colt .31-caliber six-shooter with "H. Gaebel, N.Y. 7th L. V." engraved on the backstrap. In New York City eleven days after Confederate General Beauregard had sent the first shell bursting over Fort Sumter in Charleston Harbor to begin the Civil War, Prussian-born engineer F. A. H. Gaebel was mustered into the Seventh New York Volunteer Infantry as Captain of Company A. Two months later Gaebel was leading his company against Confederate fortifications at Big Bethel, a few miles west of Newport News, Virginia. On March 8–9, 1862, during the time of the famous battle between the *Monitor* and the *Merrimac,* Gaebel and his regiment lined the northern shore of the James River and showered the Confederate ironclad monster, *Merrimac,* with rifle balls in the futile hope of doing some accidental damage to the ship's crew. In the following months the Seventh, as a part of General McClellan's vast invading army, pushed the Rebel forces behind the siege lines of Richmond.

On the opposite page are ten different types of muster rolls—a small example of the variety of data available from the National Archives. Courtesy of the National Archives. ▶

Ap 85 N.Y.

Chauncey S. Aldrich

Rank Adjutant   Reg't N.Y. Infantry.

Appears on

Field and Staff Muster Roll

for *Jany & Feby*, 1862

Present or absent *Present*

A 85 N.Y.

Chauncey S. Aldrich

Capt., Co. B, 85 Reg't N.Y. Infantry.

Appears on

Company Muster Roll

for *Sept & Oct*, 186 3

Present or absent *Present*

Ap 85 N.Y.

Chauncey S. Aldrich

Adjt., Co. , 85 Reg't N.Y. Infantry.

Appears on **Special Muster Roll**

for *Aug 18*, 1862

Present or absent *Present*

---

a 85 N.Y.

C S Aldrich

Capt, Co. B, 85 Reg't N.Y. Infantry.

Appears on **Regimental Return**

for *Oct*, 186 3

Present or absent *Present*

A 85 N.Y.

Chauncey S. Aldrich

1st Lt., Co. B, 85 Reg't N.Y. Infantry.

Age 27 years.

Appears on

Company Muster-in Roll

A 85 N.Y.

Chauncey S. Aldrich

Capt., Co. B., 85 Reg't N.Y. Infantry.

Appears on a

Detachment Muster Roll

of the organization named above

for *Jan & Feb*, 1864.

Station *Canandaigua N.Y.*

Present or absent *Present*

Stoppage, $ .... 100 for

Due Gov't , $ .... 100 for

Remarks: *En Command of Company until Feb 16 1864. — Detached on recruiting service Feb 19 1864 by Special Order No. 44, Hd Qrs. Dept. Virginia & North Carolina*

Bookmark :

(844)   a J Anderson   Copyist.

A 85 N.Y.

J. C. Aldrich

Rank Adjt., 85 Reg't N.Y. Infantry.

Appears on

Field and Staff Muster-out Roll

of the organization named above. Roll dated

New Berne N.C., June 27 1865

Muster-out to date   * *June 27*, 1865

Last paid to   , 186

---

a 85 N.Y.

Chauncey B. Aldrich

1st Lt., Co. , 85 Reg't N.Y. Infantry.

Appears on an

Individual Muster-out Roll

---

a 85 N.Y.

Chauncey S. Aldrich

Capt., Co. B, 85 Reg't N.Y. Infantry.

Appears on **Co. Muster-out Roll**, dated

New Berne, N.C., June 2, 1865.

Muster-out to date   , 186 .

Last paid to   , 186 .

Clothing account:

Last settled   , 186 ; drawn since $ 100

Due soldier $ .... 100; due U. S. $ 100

Am't for cloth'g in kind or money adv'd $ ... 100

Due U. S. for arms, equipments, &c., $ 100

Bounty paid $ .... 100; due $ 100

Remarks: *Promoted to 1st Lieut Aug. 26, 61, Promoted to Capt. Aug. 21, 63. Discharged Dec. 15, 64 under provisions of paragraph 3, Circular 75, A.G. Office series of 64*

Book mark :

(861)   Jno. J. Bell, Jr.   Copyist.

---

a 85 N.Y.

Chauncey S. Aldrich

Adjutant 85 Reg NY Vols

Return

of the Post of Newport News, Va.,

for the month of *September*, 1862,

dated   *Oct 3*, 1862,

shows the following with regard to the person named above :

By now Gaebel's bravery had caused him to be promoted to major. For three more months and five more battles—Peach Orchard, Savage Station, White Oak Swamp, Malvern Hill (where he was breveted for bravery in action), and South Mountain—Major Gaebel's luck held, and for all his recklessness he remained untouched by shell or bullet. Then, on September 16, at the Battle of Antietam, called Sharpsburg by the Rebels, a Confederate Minié ball struck him down for the first time. On December 13, not yet fully recovered from his Antietam wound, he led his regiment up the shell- and shrapnel-swept Marye's Heights at Fredericksburg. On this bloody slope over 7,000 Union soldiers were to lie dead or wounded. A medical report from the National Archives shows that Gaebel's index finger was broken when a bullet smashed his sword from his hand. A musket ball pierced his body, and a shell fragment tore a hole in his leg. Totally disabled but still alive and now a lieutenant colonel, he was sent back to his native New York City to convalesce. Several months later he left a bride of one month to return to duty with the Seventh until it was mustered out of service in May, 1863. Too crippled for active service, he volunteered as a major in the Sixteenth Veteran's Reserve Corps, a regiment made up of invalids like himself. As the commanding officer of this group, he spent the remainder of the war chasing draft dodgers, escaped prisoners, and Southern sympathizers in the mountains of Pennsylvania. At one time the government records show that he and his regiment were tracking down suspected assassins of Abraham Lincoln. After Appomattox, the federal government honored Gaebel by giving him a first lieutenant's commission in the Forty-fifth Regiment of the regular United States Army. Three years

---

Colt .31-caliber six-shooter carried by Colonel H. Gaebel when he led his regiment in a disastrous charge up Marye's Heights in the battle of Fredericksburg, Virginia, December 11–15, 1862. This information was found by a special request for medical records in the National Archives—an easy search because all the necessary preliminary information was plainly engraved on the pictured backstrap.

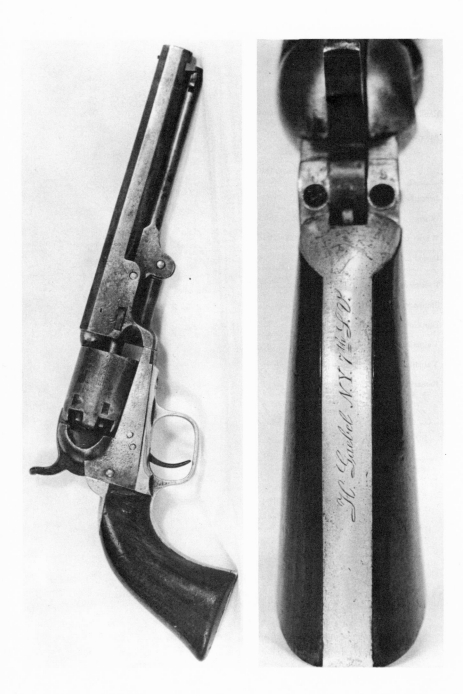

G. | 7th | **N. Y.**

F. A. H. Gaebel

Rank Lt. Col., 7. Reg't N. Y. Infantry.

Appears on

Field and Staff Muster Roll

for Jan. & Feb., 186 3.

Joined for duty and enrolled:

When Sept. 28, 186 2.*

Where Camp near Fallmouth Va

Period .... years.*

Present or absent Absent

Stoppage, $........ 100 for ....

Due Gov't, $........ 100 for 100

Valuation of horse, $........... 100

Valuation of horse equipments, $........... 100

Remarks: Wounded in battle of Fredricksburg Oct. 13. In Hospital at Washington.

* ☞ See enrollment on card from muster-in roll.

Book mark : ....

(857c)   E. E. Rankin,
                              Copyist.

Vet. Res. Corps. Nov 12/63. Brevted Lt. Col. U. S. V. Dec. 10"/64. Gunshot in right side, gunshot in hilt of sword breaking index finger, puice of shell cutting the right leg. degree of disability Total.

Above is an officer's muster roll from the National Archives for Lt. Col. F. A. H. Gaebel, 7th New York Infantry. It shows that he was "Wounded in [the] battle of Fredricksburg October 13" and was in the hospital in Washington. Often you can dig deeper beyond such a brief reporting of the facts, as the author did, and come up with the fascinating details, as can be seen by the accompanying report. Courtesy of the National Archives.

A. A. Pro. Mar. Gen'ls Office
Harrisburg, Pa. June 1st 1865

Special Order
   No. 22

       Bv't Lt. Col. F. A. H. Gaebel, Commd'g.
16th Regt. Vet. Res Corps, is hereby directed to proceed
without delay to Clearfield County, and make a
thorough investigation of certain cases in which
he alleges, that evidence may be found to implicate
parties in the conspiracy, to assasinate the
President
       The Quartermasters Department will furnish
the necessary transportation.

            (Signed)   E. W. Hinks.
                   Brig'r Gen'l 26. S. Vols.
                      A. A. Pro. Mar. Gen'l.

A. true Copy

1st Lt. Co. C. 16th V. R. C.
and Adjutant

This order directs Lt. Col. F. A. H. Gaebel of the 16th Veteran's Reserve Corps to investigate persons suspected of being involved in the assassination of Abraham Lincoln. Such a find makes a search unusually rewarding, especially if the soldier was a close relative. Courtesy of the National Archives.

later Gaebel's old war wounds sapped his strength and he died just before Christmas in 1868.

Many aspects of this story were found by using GSA 6751 forms and requesting medical records in addition to regular military records.

Here, then, is what you may expect from form GSA 6751: for the Union soldier, pension, military, medical, and court-martial records; for the Confederate soldier, as a general rule, military records only. These may include muster rolls, leaves, perhaps a prisoner-of-war record, and a few miscellaneous orders. You will have to turn to the individual state archives for more information on Johnny Reb. The National Archives, however, are the ultimate source for Union military personnel records and for tens of millions of historical facts concerning both the Union and the Confederate armies and navies.

One last hopeful hint in using GSA 6751. The training and ability of the government's searchers varies considerably. If your form is returned to you with the discouraging message, "We were unable to complete your order" or "Records searched but not found," your searcher may have had an off day or been new to the job or whatever. Just send in another set with the same information. Your new request may fall into some expert hands that can find exactly what you were requesting. It has happened to me!

Those of you who have either a microfilm reader or easy access to one will be glad to learn that the National Archives has for sale a paperback book entitled *List of National Archives Microfilm Publications*. Here are listed thousands of microfilm rolls of records from the Secretary of War, Judge Advocate's office, Chief Signal Officer, military posts, and navy personnel, to mention only a bare fraction of the entries. These records are not limited to the Civil War but cover all aspects of American history from the Revolution to well into the twentieth century. The casual searcher will not often need to use microfilm. A serious Civil War student must not overlook microfilm from the archives if he does not have the time and money to visit Washington himself.

3 / The State Archives

A bottomless well of information the National Ar-
chives may be, but there are, nevertheless, countless other sources
to which you may turn. Let us go next to the state archives. They
are full to the brim with records of servicemen who fought in
what many Southerners preferred to call "The War for Southern
Independence" and ardent Northerners termed "The War of the
Rebellion."

Each state in the nation has archives in which the state's historical treasures and records are kept. Some states, such as Michigan, Virginia, and Georgia, have superb facilities. Others appar-
ently care less for their past or are unable to obtain the necessary
funds, and their archives and offers of help reflect this. Varied in
quality as the help is, most of the states will be able to add something to your search.

There are a number of advantages that do not seem apparent
at first in writing to the state. If you are really anxious for a quick
answer to a few basic questions, such as "Does a record of my
soldier really exist (there are thousands that don't)?" What
were his service dates, promotions, and unit?" or "Did he die in
the war?" then the state archives are your best bet. A letter ad-
dressed to a state government will bring a reply in from one to
three weeks at most. A request to the harassed and understaffed
National Archives in Washington will take from one to three
months.

If your soldier happens to be a Confederate, it is really essen-
tial to write to the state in whose forces he served. Years after the
War Between the States was over, the federal government gave
pensions to most of those who had fought in the Union armies.
But after fighting a long and disastrous war, the federal government was understandably not in the mood to give pensions to
soldiers of the Confederacy, so recently the enemy. So it was that
Confederate pensions were left to the consciences of the ex-Con-

federate governments. The result was that each Southern state gave its own individual pensions to its soldiers. When Johnny Rebs sat down in courthouses throughout the South to fill out their pension forms, they were, without realizing it, contributing considerably to the preservation of their wartime history. Years later, to the delight of relatives, collectors, and historians, Confederate pension records proved to be a small mine of information.

As an example, the Louisiana "Soldier's Application for Pension" gives the applicant's age, place of birth, date of enlistment, command and company, and branch of service. It will tell whether the veteran was wounded, where, when, and during what battle, how he was wounded, the nature of the wound, and the attending surgeon. If he was a prisoner of war, the pension application will tell when and how he was released, whether he was paroled or discharged, whether he suffered the loss of an eye or a limb, and whether he was discharged for wounds or disability. It will also tell whether the soldier was at the final surrender or took the oath of allegiance to the United States during the war. It will tell whether he was married, how many children he had, what his occupation was after the war, and whether he owned any real estate. It will even state whether or not he drank. In addition, it will name two comrades and give their addresses.

If the soldier you are tracing, whether Union or Confederate, was in the State Militia and not a volunteer, he will have no records in Washington. They will be only in the state archives.

A word about the difference between the State Militia and the State Volunteers. The militia was a state-organized and controlled citizen army, now called the National Guard, whose main purpose was to protect the citizens and property within a particular state. The militia had no connection with either the Confederate or Union governments. During the Civil War both Union and Confederate militia troops often left their state to fight for their country. However, almost all of the vast armies on both sides were made up mostly of State Volunteer regiments, raised and turned over to Abe Lincoln or Jeff Davis. For those

DECLARATION FOR ORIGINAL INVALID PENSION.

State of New York,
County of *New York* {s.s.:

On this *3d* day of *December* 187*9*, personally appeared before me

CLERK OF *N. Y. Supreme* COURT, a duly authorized officer

of a Court of Record in the County and State aforesaid, *Thomas Cummings*

who being duly sworn according to law, declares:—That he is the identical person who enlisted under the name ~~of~~

aforesaid in the military service of the United States at *New York*

on the *21st* day of *May, 1861* in Company *"76"* of the *82nd*

Regiment, *New York*

in the war of 1861, and was honorably discharged on the *25th* day of *June, 1864*

That while in the service aforesaid, and in the line of his duty, he *was wounded in the right thigh, about midway between the knee and hip, at the battle of Gettysburg, Pa., on July 2nd 1863. The ball entered in front, towards the outside of the leg and passed straight through from front to rear.*

He was treated for two or three days in West's Building Hospital, Baltimore Md., was then furloughed for thirty days, and the furlough was extended for five days by the Medical Director at New York City.

At the time of his wounding he was Captain of the above company.

That he has not been employed in the Military or Naval Service of the United States, otherwise than as above stated.

He has never received or applied for pension, for which he now applies, under act of Congress approved July 14th,

1862, and amendments, by reason of the disability above stated.

He hereby constitutes and appoints *Theo. D. Valentine* ~~X. P. Brock~~, No. 111 Nassau Street, New York, his Attorney to prosecute

this claim, with full power of substitution and revocation.

A New York State Invalid Pension form showing that Capt. Thomas Cummings of the 82nd Regiment was "wounded in the right thigh midway between the knee and hip at the battle of Gettysburg, Pa. . . . The ball entered in front, towards the outside of the leg and passed straight through from front to rear." Many veterans have such details of their wounds recorded in the National Archives in Washington. Courtesy of the National Archives.

tracing earlier soldiers who were in militia units in the War of 1812 and during the Indian Wars, if their units were not officially taken into the army, their records will be found in the state files only. Revolutionary soldiers are the exception. All the available records of soldiers, sailors, and marines of Washington's troops and ships can be found in the National Archives.

After the war, a number of Confederate state officials, still bitter and unreconstructed, deliberately withheld records requested by the federal authorities. So here is another reason why more information is not available in Washington.

Some years ago the federal government began reproducing on microfilm all the veterans' personnel records held in the National Archives. This giant task began and ended with Southern soldiers. It included not only records of Johnny Rebs but those of Southern men who were against disunion and marched north to join the Blue ranks. So far, the Northern personnel records have not been reproduced, nor are there any plans to do so. Libraries and state archives throughout the South have purchased copies of the microfilmed records, and they are available to you on request at about the same cost as those of the National Archives. Check the list of addresses in Appendix A to locate those records nearest you. You will probably save a month or perhaps two that you would otherwise spend in waiting for replies from Washington.

The federal government has also compiled an index to these Southern records which you may find useful. It will give all the recorded names and regiments of all the soldiers from Southern states who fought in either army. With this index you can establish whether records exist on any soldier of Southern origin. This index has been sold all over the United States to colleges, universities, state and local historical societies, and archives. Appendix B lists where these indexes may be found.

Most of the states involved in the Civil War will send a brief abstract of a particular soldier at no cost to you. Those states that have the staff and equipment will usually go into a deeper search

CHARLOTTE CAPERS
DIRECTOR

September 9, 1965

Mr. Bertram H. Groene
P. O. Box 611
Tallahassee, Florida

Dear Mr. Groene:

      Your letter of September 2 to the Adjutant General
has been forwarded to this Department for reply. In compliance
with your request, we have made a careful search through the
Official Confederate Military Records on file in this Department
for the record of George W. Bigham.

      We have found that he served as a Captain in Company F
of the Twenty-sixth Regiment of Mississippi Infantry, CSA. I
regret that we cannot offer you any further information concerning this man. The Official Confederate Military Records on file
in this Department contain only the name, rank, and organization
of each soldier. It is possible that you might secure additional
information concerning this man by writing to the War Records
Division, National Archives, Washington, D. C.

      Whenever this Department can be of further service to
you, please do not fail to call upon us.

Sincerely yours,

Charlotte Capers

Charlotte Capers

CC:s
enclosure

---

*Sometimes state archives can offer you much information. Sometimes,
however, try as they may, they can find only rather meagre facts, as
the above letter indicates.*

at fifteen cents or more a page for duplicated records. From those states equipped to help you, you may get quite a bit on individual soldiers and military units. I must sadly relate that such states as Louisiana, which will go beyond summaries in response to a mail request for information, are growing fewer by the year. Almost all the states are quite eager for you to come and look for yourself into their extensive archives and use them. Lack of money for a research staff, however, is gradually limiting mail searches. Many of the states, such as Michigan, North Carolina, and Arkansas, will send you special pamphlets on the contents of their archives.

Remember, when tracing Yankees or Rebels, a letter will get better results than a hasty card. Send your inquiry to one of the state addresses given below:

ALABAMA: Military Records Division
Department of Archives and History
State of Alabama
Montgomery, Alabama 36130

ARKANSAS: Arkansas History Commission
Old State House
Little Rock, Arkansas 72201

CALIFORNIA: California State Archives
Archives Building
1020 O Street
Sacramento, California 95814

COLORADO: Division of State Archives
and Public Records
1313 Sherman Street
Denver, Colorado 80203

CONNECTICUT: The Adjutant General
Attention: Records Officer
State Armory
360 Broad Street
Hartford, Connecticut 06115
or

Connecticut State Library
231 Capitol Avenue
Hartford, Connecticut 06115

DELAWARE: Public Archives Commission
Dover, Delaware 19901

FLORIDA: Department of State
Division of Archives, History
and Records Management
The Capitol
Tallahassee, Florida 32304

GEORGIA: Georgia Department of Archives
and History
Civil War Records Section
330 Capitol Avenue, SW
Atlanta, Georgia 30334

ILLINOIS: The Director
Archives-Records Management Division
Office of the Secretary of State
Springfield, Illinois 62706

INDIANA: Archives and Records Management
Division
Military Records
Indiana State Library
140 North Senate Avenue
Indianapolis, Indiana 46204

IOWA: Iowa State Historical Department
Division of Historical Museum
and Archives
East 12th and Grand Avenue
Des Moines, Iowa 50319

KANSAS: Kansas State Historical Society
10th and Jackson Streets
Topeka, Kansas 66612

*KENTUCKY: Kentucky Historical Society
Old State House
P.O. Box H
Frankfort, Kentucky 40601

LOUISIANA: Director
Louisiana State Archives
   and Records Service
Secretary of State
P.O. Box 44125 Capitol
Baton Rouge, Louisiana 70804

MAINE: State of Maine
Maine State Archives
L-M-A Building
Augusta, Maine 04333

MARYLAND: Archivist, State of Maryland
Department of General Services
Hall of Records
P.O. Box 828
Annapolis, Maryland 21404

MASSACHUSETTS: The Commonwealth of Massachusetts
Military Division
The Adjutant General's Office
War Records Section, Room 1000
100 Cambridge Street
Boston, Massachusetts 02202

*No research by mail. Will send list of genealogists on request.

MICHIGAN:	State Archives Michigan History Division 3405 N. Logan Street Lansing, Michigan 48918
MINNESOTA:	Reference Services Division of Archives and Manuscripts Minnesota Historical Society 1500 Mississippi Street St. Paul, Minnesota 55101
MISSISSIPPI:	Department of Archives and History P.O. Box 571 Jackson, Mississippi 39205
MISSOURI:	Adjutant General's Office Industrial Drive Jefferson City, Missouri 65101
NEVADA:	Secretary of State Division of Archives Carson City, Nevada 89701
NEW HAMPSHIRE:	The Adjutant General of New Hampshire State Military Reservation 1 Airport Road Concord, New Hampshire 03301
NEW JERSEY:	Archives and History Bureau New Jersey State Library 185 West State Street Trenton, New Jersey 08625
NEW MEXICO:	State Records Center and Archives 404 Montezuma Santa Fe, New Mexico 87501

NEW YORK: Bureau of War Records
Division of Military and Naval Affairs
Public Security Building
State Campus
Albany, New York 12226

NORTH CAROLINA: The Search Room, Archives Branch
Division of Archives and History
Department of Cultural Resources
109 E. Jones Street
Raleigh, North Carolina 27611

*OHIO: Director
Division of Soldiers' Claims—Veterans'
   Affairs
Adjutant General's Department
State House Annex
Columbus, Ohio 43215

OKLAHOMA: Director
Research Library
Oklahoma Historical Society
Historical Building
Oklahoma City, Oklahoma 73105

PENNSYLVANIA: Director
Pennsylvania Historical and Museum
   Commission
Archives Building
Box 1076
Harrisburg, Pennsylvania 17108

RHODE ISLAND: Adjutant General's Office
1051 North Main Street
Providence, Rhode Island 02903

SOUTH CAROLINA: South Carolina Department
   of Archives and History

*No research by mail. Will send list of genealogists on request.

P.O. Box 11
669 Capitol Station
Columbia, South Carolina 29211

SOUTH DAKOTA: Historical Resources Center
Memorial Building
Pierre, South Dakota 57501

TENNESSEE: Archives Section
Tennessee State Library
and Archives
403 7th Avenue North
Nashville, Tennessee 37219

TEXAS: Director of State Archives
Texas State Library
Box 12927 Capitol Station
Austin, Texas 78711

VERMONT: Director
State Office of Veterans' Affairs
City Hall Building
Montpelier, Vermont 05602

VIRGINIA: Archives Division
Virginia State Library
Richmond, Virginia 23219

WEST VIRGINIA: West Virginia Department
of Archives and History
Science and Cultural Center
Capitol Complex
Charleston, West Virginia 25305

WISCONSIN: Archives Division
The State Historical Society
of Wisconsin
816 State Street
Madison, Wisconsin 53706

4 / The OR and the ORN

If you consider your search for a Civil War ancestor complete once your letters have exhausted the information in the state and national archives, you are in for a very happy surprise. What may be one of the most exciting and rewarding parts of your search lies ahead of you. You must face the fact that, extremely valuable and indispensable as the state and national personnel records are, most of them are quite brief, completely impersonal, and as mechanical as a robot's diary: enlisted, promoted, absent on leave, sick, discharged, captured, pensioned, died.

There are thousands upon thousands of records, both official and unofficial, that are not found in a soldier's personnel file. These records vary from the precise and detailed battle reports and correspondence of the *Official Records* to the vivid and compelling stories of soldiers as found in diaries, personal narratives, and the histories of the regiments in which they served.

By far the most important set of books in print is the huge 128-volume *Official Records of the Union and Confederate Armies in the War of the Rebellion*, popularly called the *OR* by Civil War scholars. In 1864 the United States government began collecting all the available Union armies' records, reports, orders, and memorandums ever issued, posted, filed, or printed. After the war the federal government collected all the similar Confederate records. By 1881 Washington had begun the tremendous job of printing the more important of these records. Nineteen years later, the job was complete—128 volumes containing over 138,000 pages of records.

A companion set is the *Official Records of the Union and Confederate Navies in the War of the Rebellion*, or the *ORN*. Begun in 1894, it took twenty-eight years to complete the thirty-one volumes. These two sets, the *OR* and the *ORN*, together with an accompanying Atlas, famous for its accuracy and size, make up the most used and quoted set of Civil War records in existence.

This is due to their reliability, vast coverage, and availability. Most large city libraries, all state universities, and many smaller colleges have both the *OR* and the *ORN,* and they are there for anyone to use. These records have also been duplicated on microfilm.

In any Civil War research the *OR* and the *ORN* are really indispensable. They give firsthand reports written by ships' captains, regimental colonels, and brigade commanders who directed and took part in the great land battles and naval engagements of the war. If great-grandfather's regiment was in any noteworthy fighting, there is a good chance that what he saw will be retold by other men who were there, if not by great-grandfather himself. The story may be a bit biased, for in many cases an officer's report was a defense of his own actions. Most of the time, however, it will be close to the truth as he saw it and perhaps as great-grandfather fought it. The chances of your relative's name being specifically mentioned in the *OR* or the *ORN* will depend upon his rank. This is because enlisted men did the fighting, not the organizing, directing, and reporting of the fighting. That was the officers' job. Generals are frequently mentioned, and their reports are often printed. You can shake thousands of colonels and hundreds of navy captains out of the *OR* and the *ORN.* As the rank decreases, an officer's chance of survival in print decreases.

It is remarkable, though, just how many men of lower ranks and grades are mentioned by name. It is this fact that gives the single 1,242-page *OR* Index and the smaller 475-page *ORN* Index a special significance. If you know only great-grandfather's name and not the state in which he enlisted or the regiment in which he fought, or if the Civil War soldier's letter you possess has no identification other than a signature, there is a fair chance of associating that name with a regiment, ship, or state. Just look up the name in the *OR* or the *ORN* Index.

These two indexes are extremely useful, but there is a small trick in learning how to use them. Suppose you find a letter signed by Paul J. Semmes. In the *OR* Index you will find, listed after his name, I, 11, 12, 19, 21, 25, 27, 29, 51; III, 1; IV, 1. The 128 *OR* books are divided into four parts, called series. They are I, II, III, and IV. So the I, III, and IV indicate that references to Semmes will be found in Series I, III, and IV. The numbers after the Roman numerals are volume numbers, not page numbers. I, 11 means that in Series I and in volume eleven's own separate index in the back of the book you will find the name, Paul J. Semmes, and the pages in that particular volume where he is mentioned. Be sure to note that the general index has a section on additions and corrections.

In the summer of 1971 the National Historical Society of Gettysburg, Pennsylvania, printed a thousand copies of the *OR* set. Shortly before this, the National Archives began publishing *A Guide-Index to the Official Records of the Union and Confederate Armies, 1861–1865*. The guide is being put out in bits and pieces, called "Fascicles," or chapters. This new index, although not absolutely necessary to the "soldier hunter," has its uses. You may wish information on the battle of Malvern Hill, Virginia. In Volume II, section L, page 39, you will find (1) reference to the pages in *The Official Atlas of the Civil War* on which maps of Malvern Hill appear; (2) listing of volumes and pages that contain the official reports of all military action in the area; (3) Union reports by various officers; (4) Confederate reports by various officers; (5) any Union and Confederate correspondence mentioning the area. It lists all the entries concerning this battle within the space of less than half a page. It would take a trained professional historian at least a full day to search out all these references without the aid of the *Guide-Index*. The *Index* is gradually coming off the press, so be patient and the wait will be worth it. You can order it from the United States Government Printing Office.

Massive and comprehensive as the 160 volumes of the *OR* and the *ORN* appear, they are still only the small visible part of the giant iceberg of historical nonpersonal documents, the great bulk of which is hidden unpublished under the surface in the National

Archives in Washington. The nonpersonal military records are a little more inaccessible than is the information in great-grandfather's military service record jacket or in his pension file. These millions of documents contain every conceivable type of military information and are concerned with everything from one-man details to one-hundred-thousand-man armies, and from naval buoys to naval stations and battleships. Naturally, the vast Union forces are covered more thoroughly than those of the Confederacy. Even at that, the federal government is the chief repository for most Confederate records. You can travel pretty far into these records with writing paper and checkbook. Here you will not be searching directly for great-grandfather, but for his regiment and his battles, or his ship and his cruise.

A request for specific information, not a form this time, to the **Military Service Records (NNCC), National Archives (GSA), Washington, D.C. 20408,** will bring a reply in a month or two. If Archives and Records can help you, it will usually be to acquaint you with records that they can duplicate or with microfilm that you may purchase from them.

Let's suppose that your relative was a sailor. Suppose also that you have exhausted his personnel folder and his pension and medical records and that you have squeezed your local library's *ORN* for every scrap of information concerning his ship, the Union ironclad *Keokuk,* sunk in Charleston Harbor in April, 1863. Next, you would send a letter to Archives and Records, requesting further information. The reply would inform you that a copy of a muster roll of the *Keokuk* was available for sale and three rolls of microfilm concerning the ship, as well. Many of the archives' records are for sale on microfilm. Fortunately, you do not need to own a microfilm reader, even though they are becoming fairly inexpensive. Most libraries of even moderate size own at least one microfilm reader, and it is a rare librarian who will refuse you the use of one. If you plan on any extensive use of the National Archives, the *List of National Archives Microfilm Publications* mentioned on page 24 is particularly helpful. It not only lists and gives the price of all of the government's records available on microfilm, but it has a number of very handy order forms in the back.

It may be that you will have to search the National Archives beyond the end of the war in 1865. This is because many Civil War veterans served on beyond the end of the war in regular United States Army regiments or aboard United States Navy ships and stations. The National Archives Personnel Records are limited mainly to the following years:

United States Army   1775–1912
United States Navy   1776–1885
United States Marines 1798–1895

For personnel records beyond these dates you should write to the army or navy personnel departments, Washington, D.C.

One unusual example of service after the Civil War was that of General Joe Wheeler. Wheeler was a major general of Confederate cavalry. At the end of the war he was imprisoned with ex-President Jefferson Davis as a dangerous enemy leader whom many wanted hanged. Any type of reasoning would come to the conclusion that Wheeler's military career had come to a complete and disastrous end. Thirty-three years later Confederate General Wheeler was Major General Wheeler, United States Army, directing American troops as they charged up the slopes of a hill near Santiago, Cuba, in the Spanish-American War. The story goes that, when the Spanish line broke and ran before his advancing regiments, he forgot time and place and shouted after his charging troopers, "After 'em, boys! We've got the Yankees on the run!"

Any number of Union men remained in the Federal army after the war. There were even Confederate prisoners who joined the Union Army during the war. They joined, not as deserters or turncoats but as Indian fighters, and were labeled "Galvanized Yankees," the idea being that just as a sheet of galvanized iron is covered with a thin layer of zinc, so the ex-Confederate was galvanized with a thin layer of "official Yankee," blue coat and all. Underneath, however, lay a hard-core Rebel. Some of these "Galvanized Yankees" remained in the army after the war.

This all goes to point up the fact that your veteran may have had a service career after the end of the great Civil War, and he may even have served on both sides. Such service would be indicated through a pension file record or a notation of enlistment in the regular United States Army found in the soldier's personnel file. The Navy, especially, grew in size after the war, and a good many Civil War bluejackets' records extend on toward the turn of the century.

5 / Your Guide to Millions of Pages

There is yet more beyond the OR, the ORN, the giant miscellaneous holdings of the National Archives, and the holdings of the various states. There are books, rosters, and regimental histories by the tens of thousands. For these one must turn to the library. Here, in public and private collections across the country, are deposited books, articles, memoirs, diaries, and journals on the war. The library at your state capital or larger university will often be your best help. If you are too far from either of these, your hometown library will do. A library can borrow books from any part of the nation through a system called "Interlibrary Loan."

Your first concern will be to find a really good guide to the endless amount of Civil War literature scattered across the United States. The books that will be your guides to these new sources are known as bibliographies. They contain lists of Civil War publications by subject, title, and author. Since 1865 quite a few of these bibliographies have been published. There are, however, two guides on the market today that have no equal. The first is *Civil War Books: A Critical Bibliography,* by Allan Nevins, James I. Robertson, Jr., and Bell I. Wiley. It is in two volumes and is published by the Louisiana State University Press. These two volumes list almost all the significant as well as many of the insignificant Civil War books printed from the 1850's to the 1960's. They give a brief statement about the contents of each book and also contain helpful comments about the book's accuracy and completeness. Let us suppose that in your research you are referred to Rufus R. Dawes' *Service with the Sixth Wisconsin Volunteers.* A quick look in "Nevins, Robertson, and Wiley" will tell you that this book is "the best narrative by a soldier from the Midwest; based on the author's letters and diary, the work is

Davenport, Alfred.
Camp and field life of the Fifth New York volunteer infantry. (Duryee zouaves.) By Alfred Davenport New York, Dick and Fitzgerald, 1879.

485 p. front. (port.) pl. 19½ᶜᵐ

This thoroughly useful narrative, based on diaries and letters, covers admirably the exploits of a regiment that saw valiant service through Chancellorsville.

Davidson, Henry M   *d.* 1900.
History of Battery A. First regiment of Ohio vol. light artillery. Milwaukee, Daily Wisconsin steam printing house, 1865.

vii, [9]–199 p. 19½ᶜᵐ.

A cursory, early account, based largely on company records, alleged diaries, and the author's own recollections.

Davis, Charles E   *b.* 1842 or 1843–1915.
Three years in the army. The story of the Thirteenth Massachusetts volunteers from July 16, 1861, to August 1, 1864. By Charles E. Davis, jr. Boston, Estes and Lauriat, 1894.

xxxv, 476 p. maps. 23½ cm.

Five diaries and numerous official sources formed the basis for this highly regarded history of a unit that served in the Army of the Potomac until its disbandment in the summer of 1864.

Davis, Nicholas A
The campaign from Texas to Maryland. By Rev. Nicholas A. Davis ... Richmond. Printed at the office of the Presbyterian committee of publication of the Confederate States. 1863.

165, [1] p. 2 port. (incl. front.) 19½ᶜᵐ.

One of the better narratives treating of Hood's Texas Brigade; contains personal comments on almost all aspects of the war.

Davis, Nicholas A
Chaplain Davis and Hood's Texas Brigade. Edited and with an introd. by Donald E. Everett. San Antonio, Principia Press of Trinity University, 1962.

284 p. 24 cm.

A vastly expanded version, with good editorial trappings added, of Davis's Campaign from Texas . . .

Davis, Oliver Wilson
Life of David Bell Birney, major-general United States volunteers. Philadelphia, King & Baird; New York, Sheldon & co., 1867.

xii, 418 p. front. (port.) 26ᶜᵐ

Its eulogistic passages notwithstanding, this military biography is a basic source for any study of the Army of the Potomac.

Davis, William Watts Hart, 1820–1910.
History of the 104th Pennsylvania regiment, from August 22nd, 1861, to September 30th, 1864. By W. W. H. Davis ... Philadelphia, J. B. Rogers, printer, 1866.

vii, 1 l., 9–364 p. incl. front. pl., port. 23 cm.

Col. Davis entered the Civil War with the intention of writing his unit's history, and the resulting study is a highly reliable commentary on the Peninsular and Carolina coastal campaigns.

Dawes, Rufus R 1838–1899.
Service with the Sixth Wisconsin volunteers. By Rufus R. Dawes ... Marietta, O., E. R. Alderman & sons, 1890.

2 p. l., v, [5]–330 p. front., illus., port. 22½ᶜᵐ.

The best narrative by a soldier from the Midwest; based on the author's letters and diary, the work is a standard source for the Eastern battles and the Iron Brigade.

Dawes, Rufus R 1838–1899.
Service with the Sixth Wisconsin Volunteers. Edited with an introd. by Alan T. Nolan. Madison, State Historical Society of Wisconsin for Wisconsin Civil War Centennial Commission, 1962.

xv, 330 (i. e. 336) p. illus., ports. 23 cm.

A needed reissue of the original, with a revealing introduction and critical bibliography.

Dawson, Francis W
Reminiscences of Confederate service, 1861–1865. By Capt. Francis W. Dawson ... Charleston, S. C., The News and courier book presses, 1882.

180 p. 23½ᶜᵐ.

Dawson was an Englishman who served on Longstreet's staff and afterwards became the internationally known editor of the Charleston Courier; a penetrating commentary, deserving of republication.

A page from Civil War Books, *by Nevins, Robertson, and Wiley. This is one of the most important library guides you will use in your search of a regimental history.*

a standard source for the Eastern battles and the Iron Brigade."
Suppose another one of your references is a pamphlet by William
H. Clark entitled "Reminiscences of the Thirty-fourth Regiment, Massachusetts Volunteer Infantry." *Civil War Books* will
tell you that this work is "little more than a footnote on the 1864
battle of New Market, Va." Such comments will help you decide
whether you want to get a work through interlibrary loan, and
they may save you from buying the book sight unseen and being
disappointed when you receive it. *Civil War Books* is available
in bookstores and in most libraries.

The second and by far the most complete guide to regimental
publications and personal narratives is Charles E. Dornbusch's
Military Bibliography of the Civil War, in three volumes. They
are published by the New York Public Library, Fifth Avenue
and 42nd Street, New York, N. Y. 10018. This set is also available
by sending your order to C. E. Dornbusch, Hope Farm Press and
Book Shop, Strong Road, Cornwallville, N.Y. 12418. Dornbusch
lists practically every book ever written about military units,
both Northern and Southern, and includes, as well, most of the
articles concerned with regimental histories that are to be found
in journals and in the leading professional history magazines. It
is an invaluable work. It is not expensive and can be obtained or
ordered in any bookstore. Suppose you know of an ancestor who
was in the Twenty-first Ohio Infantry. Dornbusch lists each of
Ohio's regiments of cavalry, artillery, and infantry. He then pro-
ceeds to list everything that has been written concerning each of
Ohio's military units. You will find in Dornbusch that there are
one published diary, one complete history, and two articles written about the Twenty-first Ohio. If it is the Seventeenth Virginia
Infantry that you are interested in, you will find that there have

---

Here is an example from Charles E. Dornbusch's well-known
Military Bibliography of the Civil War. *This is the most important single work in print today for those searching a regiment's* ▶
*complete history. Note National Union Catalog symbols after
each item, which aid in locating each book or article.*

5TH CAVALRY

Mustered in: January 9 to May 5, 1864.

Mustered out: October 31, 1865.

Mass soldiers vi 492–544.

Mass in the war 781–3.

Bowditch, Charles Pickering
War letters of Charles P. Bowditch. *Massachusetts historical society proceedings* LVII (1923/24) 414–95. facs., plate (port.).   73

1st Battalion of Cavalry

Mustered in and attached to 26th regiment of New York cavalry: December 30, 1864 to January 2, 1865.

Mustered out: June 30, 1865.

Mass soldiers vi 545–65.

Mass in the war 784.

INFANTRY

1ST INFANTRY

Mustered in: May 23–27, 1861.

Mustered out: May 25, 1864.

Mass soldiers i 1–68.

Mass in the war 99–112.

Constitution, by laws, and rules of order of the First regiment relief association, organized, June 15, 1863. Boston, J. E. Farwell & co., printers, 1863. 9, (1) p. 14cm.   MHi   74

First regiment Massachusetts volunteer infantry veteran association. Boston, Mass., February, 1911. Fiftieth anniversary roster [Boston, 1911] [32] p. port. 23½cm.   DLC   75
Caption title.

First regiment of infantry Massachusetts volunteer militia, Colonel Robert Cowdin, commanding. In service of the United States, in answer to the President's first call for troops to suppress the rebellion, April 5, 1861. Compiled from original papers in the Adjutant general and Auditor's offices of the Commonwealth. Boston, Wright and Potter print co., 1903. 50 p. 2 plates (facs., port.). 24cm.
DLC NN   76
Unit roster [15]–50. On cover: 1st regiment infantry M.V.M., 1861. "Introduction" signed: Luke Edward Jenkins, Private Company B.

Memorial service in memory of the dead of the First regt. Massachusetts volunteer infantry, 1861–64, Faneuil hall, Boston, Mass., May 21, 1911. [16] p. 23cm.   DLC NN   77
Title from cover which includes the program. A roster of those killed in action and those who have died since the war.

Bardeen, Charles William, 1847–1924.
A little fifer's war diary, by C. W. Bardeen, formerly of Co. D., 1st Mass. vol. inf. With an introduction by Nicholas Murray Butler. Syracuse, N. Y., C. W. Bardeen, 1910. 329 p. illus., maps, ports. 24cm.   NN   78
Facsimile of the author's discharge printed on inside of back cover.

Cowdin, Robert, 1806?–1874.
Gen. Cowdin and the First Massachusetts regiment of volunteers. Boston, J. E. Farwell and co., printers, 1864. 19 p. 23cm.
DLC M MHi   79

Cudworth, Warren Handel, 1825–1883.
History of the First regiment (Massachusetts infantry), from the 25th of May, 1861, to the 25th of May, 1864, including brief references to the operations of the Army of the Potomac, by Warren H. Cudworth, Chaplain of the Regiment. . . . Boston, Walker, Fuller and co., 1866. 528 p. plates (illus.). 20cm.   DLC NN   80
Unit roster [498]–528. Coulter 103.

Cutler, Frederick Morse, 1874–
The old First Massachusetts coast artillery in war and peace, by Frederick Morse Cutler. Boston, Pilgrim press [1917] 180 p. plates (illus., ports.). 19½cm.   NN   81
Civil war 46–79.

Darling, Charles B
Historical sketch of the First regiment infantry, Massachusetts volunteer militia, compiled by Chas. B. Darling. Boston. [Alfred Mudge & Sons, printers] 1890. [40] p. illus., ports. 27½ × 35½cm.   DLC   82
Advertising matter included. On cover: Souvenir of the dedication of the new armory, June, 1890.

Frye, James A   1863–1933.
The First regiment of heavy artillery, 1844–1899. In Regiments and armories of Massachusetts, edited by Charles W. Hall, 1899 i 338–60.   83
Civil war, 344–52.

Holden, Leverett Dana, 1843–1932.
My first and last fights, delivered before the Malden club, Feb. 5, 1914. Fredericksburg to Gettysburg. Memories of the Civil war, by Leverett D. Holden. Malden, Samuel Tilden, printer [1914] 85 p. front. (port.). 16½cm.
NN   84

Kingsbury, Allen Alonzo, 1840–1862.
The hero of Medfield, containing the journals and letters of Allen Alonzo Kingsbury, of Medfield, member of Co. H, Chelsea volunteers, Mass. 1st reg., who was killed by the Rebels near Yorktown, April 26, 1862. Also, notice of the other three soldiers belonging to the same company and killed at the same time,

been two books, one history and roster, two orations, and two articles concerning the Seventeenth. You will also find that the Nineteenth Pennsylvania Cavalry had practically nothing written about it, nor did the Third North Carolina Artillery. Volume I of Dornbusch covers the southern, border, and western states and the United States Territories. Volume II covers the northern states. Volume III is especially useful in obtaining the stories of specific state military units as they fought at Gettysburg, Shiloh, and the like. In publishing his book Dornbusch not only has made it possible for anyone to search out every scrap of existing literature concerning his ancestor's regiment but has done an inestimable service to collectors of antique arms and equipment by making Civil War histories so easy to locate.

There is one little trick to getting the most out of Dornbusch. At the very end of each bibliographic entry you will find a series of capital and small letters, such as NHi, CT, TCU, RR. These are National Union Catalog symbols and refer to the particular library where these books and articles may be found. NHi is the abbreviation for New York Historical Society, CT stands for Connecticut State Library, Hartford, Connecticut, and TCU stands for the University of Chattanooga's library. Suppose you have found listed a history of the Twenty-fourth Massachusetts. The Twenty-fourth Massachusetts has after it the letters DLC and NN. DLC and NN indicate that a copy of this regimental history may be found in the Library of Congress (DLC) and in the New York Public Library (NN). Most librarians have reference books that can interpret these signs for you and will be glad to help you in your interlibrary loan hunt. If you plan to do any extensive research, you may wish to purchase a small government reference book which gives a complete list of all the librar-

---

C. E. Dornbusch's very important work not only lists all material relating to regimental histories, both North and South, but gives you page after page of personal narrative, memoirs, and diaries, as well. ▶

Union Biography and Personal Narratives

In the following section, autobiographical works are listed first under each subject; biographical works follow under heading I.

AUCHMUTY, RICHARD TYLDEN, 1831–1893.
Letters of Richard Tylden Auchmuty, Fifth corps, Army of the Potomac. Edited by E.S.A. Privately printed. [n.p., 189–] 127 p. 20cm.
NHi *1842*
NHi's copy has presentation inscription of Jan. 1895. The editor is probably the wife, Ellen Schermerhorn Auchmuty, 1837–1927.

BACON, CYRUS, 1836?–1868.
A Michigan surgeon at Chancellorsville one hundred years ago. Edited by Frank Whitehouse, Jr. and Walter M. Whitehouse. *University of Michigan medical bulletin* xxix (1963) 315–31. *1843*

BAER, GEORGE FREDERICK, 1842–1911.
Oration of George F. Baer at the unveiling of the soldiers and sailors' monument at Allentown, Penna., October 19, 1899. 8 p. 27½cm.
Title from cover. CSmH *1844*

BALL, LEVI CHANDLER, 1809–1875.
Speech on the war, by Major L. Chandler Ball, delivered at Hoosick Falls, December 9th, 1863. Washington, D. C., Chronicle print, 1893. 24 p. 23cm. DLC NB *1845*

BANKS, NATHANIEL PRENTISS, 1816–1894.
An address delivered by Maj. General N. P. Banks at the Customhouse, New Orleans, on the Fourth of July, 1865. 8 p. 22cm.
CSmH *1846*

I

Celebration of the centennial of the birth of General Nathaniel Prentice Banks, Waltham, Massachusetts, January 30, 1916. [Waltham, Waltham pub. co., printers, 1916] 31 p. front. (port.). 23cm. DNW *1847*

Department of the Gulf. Historical sketch of Major Gen. N. P. Banks' civil and military administration in Louisiana. Tenth edition. New York, 1864. 12 p. 20cm. CSmH *1848*
Text signed: P. W.

General Banks. *Illinois central magazine* II 1 (July 1913) 13–22, II 2 (August 1913) 13–18. facsim., 2 illus., port. *1849*

Harrington, Fred Harvey, 1912–
. . . Fighting politician, Major General N. P. Banks, by Fred Harvey Harrington. Philadelphia, University of Pennsylvania

press, 1948. xi, (1), 301 p. front. (port.). 23cm. NN *1849A*
At head of title: The American historical association.
"Theater of operations of Major General N. P. Banks, 1861–1862 [1863–1865"] maps, end papers.

BARLOW, FRANCIS CHANNING, 1834–1896.

I

In memoriam Francis Channing Barlow, 1834–1896. Published by the authority of the State of New York under the supervision of the New York monuments commission. Albany, J. B. Lyon co., printers, 1923. front. (port.), plates (illus., maps, ports.). 27½cm. NHi *1850*
On cover: Major-General Francis C. Barlow at Gettysburg and other battlefields.

BARLOW, JOHN WHITNEY, 1938–1914.
Personal reminiscences of the war, by Lieut. Col. John W. Barlow. *MOLLUS-Wis* I 106–19.
1851

BARNUM, HENRY ALANSON, 1833–1892.
Oration delivered by Major-General Henry A. Barnum, before the Society of the Army of the Cumberland at Detroit, Nov. 15, 1871. New York, E. S. Dodge & co., printers, 1871. 21 p. 23cm. DLC *1852*

BARTLETT, WILLIAM FRANCIS, 1840–1876.

I

A record of the dedication of the statue of Major General Francis Bartlett, a tribute of the Commonwealth of Massachusetts, May 27, 1904. Boston, Printed by Wright and Potter print. co., 1905. 82 p. plates (ports.). 24½cm. NN *1853*
The Council "ordered, that Francis Hurtubis, Jr., private secretary ·to the Governor, be authorized to edit and publish a report of the proceedings."

BAYARD, GEORGE DASHIEL, 1835–1862.

I

Bayard, Samuel John, –1879.
The life of George Dashiell Bayard . . . by Samuel J. Bayard. New York, G. P. Putnam's Sons, 1874. ix, [11]–337 p. front. (port.), 2 plates (illus., fold. map). 19½cm. CSmH *1854*

BELL, LUTHER V., 1806–1862.

I

Ellis, George Edward, 1814–1894.
Memoir of Luther V. Bell, prepared by vote of the Massachusetts historical society, by

ies and their symbols. This book is entitled *Symbols of American Libraries*. It costs $1.00 and can be obtained by writing to Card Division, Library of Congress Building, #159 Navy Yard Annex, Washington, D.C. 20541.

Mention should be made here of the works of two other authors that go hand in hand with Dornbusch. Suppose all you knew of great-grandfather was that he belonged to some Confederate outfit known as the "Flat Rock Rifles," or perhaps the "Pee Dee Wild Cats." In a two-volume work by William Amann entitled *Personnel of the Civil War,* you will find that the "Flat Rock Rifles" were Company C, Twentieth Virginia Infantry, and that the "Pee Dee Wild Cats" were Company K, Twenty-sixth North Carolina Infantry. A sampling of names will indicate just how useful Amann's book can be: "Fishing Creek Avengers," Company D, Twenty-sixth Mississippi Infantry; "Orphan Brigade," First Kentucky Brigade; "Haw River Boys," Company D, Thirty-fifth North Carolina; "Stars of Equality," Company E, Nineteenth Louisiana Infantry; "Rattlesnake Rangers," Company C, Nineteenth Battalion, Georgia Cavalry; "Bartow Yankee Killers," Company A, Twenty-third Georgia Infantry.

Many of the Northern troops went by similar names, such as "Richland County Plow Boys," Company D, Eleventh Wisconsin Infantry; "Jayhawkers," Company I, Ninth Kansas Regular Cavalry; "Volcano Blues," Company D, California Fourth Regular Infantry; "Mason's Invincibles," Company B, Eighteenth Massachusetts Regular Infantry; and "Guppy Guards," Company D, Twenty-third Wisconsin Infantry.

Thomas Yoseloff publishes Amann's book as well as a similar single volume by William Tancig entitled *Confederate Military Land Units.* Both are readily available in most libraries and are inexpensive for those building reference collections. On request, the National Archives will also supply you with the same type of information that Amann and Tancig provide.

In 1961 the Allen Publishing Company of Charlottesville, Virginia, republished an old favorite of historians, *Bibliography of State Participation in the Civil War, 1861–1866,* and there are other such volumes available. However, the books by Dornbusch and by Nevins, Robertson, and Wiley are the most important guides that you can possibly have in searching out your needle in the mountainous haystack of regimental literature of the War Between the States.

What *Military Bibliography of the Civil War* and *Civil War Books* are to the armies of that great war, *American Civil War Navies,* by Myron J. Smith, Jr., is to the Northern and Southern sea services. Published in 1972 by Scarecrow Press, Inc., Box 656, Metuchen, N.J. 08840, it is a fine one-volume bibliographic listing of almost every English language book, article, or paper of any significance published from the 1850's to 1972. There are over 2,800 entries. If you wish to add to the material you have obtained from the state or national archives or from the *ORN,* you should get a copy of this book.

A regimental history will trace a particular regiment from its mustering-in ceremony through all its battles to the final disbanding of the survivors. The histories vary tremendously in quality and usefulness. With a few rare exceptions, every regiment in both great armies, North and South, has had something of its history recorded. It may be only a few pages, as in the case of the forgotten Eightieth Illinois Infantry and the Twenty-fourth South Carolina, or it may be an extensive literature in books and magazines, as in the case of Louisiana's famous Washington Artillery or the Twentieth Maine Infantry that stepped through the gates of everlasting glory at Gettysburg.

Regimental histories are especially good for tracing the higher ranking officers—the majors, lieutenant colonels, and colonels. Almost all these histories give detailed biographies of these officers, and many include anecdotes and much personal information gathered by fellow officers and comrades at the time. More often than not these books include photographs of all the higher ranking officers in the regiment, making the regimental history a really indispensable source for searchers of these leaders.

Not so long ago I purchased a photograph of a serene-looking, much-bewhiskered Civil War officer. Signed in black ink with a firm hand across the bottom was "Col. Cilley, 1st Me. Cav." When I got home, I headed straight for my library and pulled from the shelf Dornbusch's volume containing Maine regimental histories. Here I found a searcher's dream come true. There were twenty-five separate entries, including a 735-page regimental history that contained a photograph and much information on Cilley. In addition to a second 436-page history, there were two articles written by the Colonel himself, as well as many other articles. Quite a few of the articles related to Cilley, his bravery, and his leadership.

A few months after acquiring the Cilley photograph I was able to obtain a personally autographed photograph of Confederate cavalry leader John Hunt Morgan. It was Morgan who, in July, 1863, led 2,500 grey-clad cavalrymen in a magnificent sweep into Kentucky, Indiana, and Ohio, only to be captured with his whole command. Morgan escaped from the Ohio penitentiary at Columbus where he and his officers were kept. He returned south to become one of the best-known and most dashing of all Confederate cavalry leaders until his death in September, 1864, near Greeneville, Tennessee.

In looking into the lives of better-known officers such as Morgan, you may go again to Dornbusch, who also lists biographies. Nevins, Robertson, and Wiley's *Civil War Books* will do just fine, also, in giving you a list of books to work on. Again, remember that, although Nevins, Robertson, and Wiley's *Civil War Books* parallels Dornbusch, the latter has a more complete listing and includes sources other than books. *Civil War Books,* however, has a special quality, for it gives a short critical evaluation of each of its entries, which Dornbusch does not. So take your pick. They are the best there are in their field.

Another useful book is Frederick Dyer's three-volume *A Compendium of the War of the Rebellion.* Frederick Dyer, a Connecticut drummer boy, was immensely proud of being a Northern veteran in the War of the Rebellion. He was so fiercely proud that he made it a personal obligation to write and commit to memory the histories of over 2,000 Union regiments formed between 1861 and 1865. Needless to say, Dyer was an intellectual oddity and was looked upon with wonder and amazement by fellow veterans.

In 1903, at the urging of his comrades, fifty-four-year-old Dyer began the truly awe-inspiring task of outlining the histories, commanders, and movements of all the regiments in the Union army.

Above are the photographs of the famous Confederate cavalry general, John Hunt Morgan, who invaded southern Ohio with a large force of cavalry, and lesser-known Colonel Jonathan P. Cilley, of the First Maine Cavalry, often wounded in battle and once near death. As is the case North or South, there was much information on these two men for they were officers above the rank of major. Collectors don't take much of a gamble here, for they can be reasonably certain to find more than a little information.

Working constantly and alone, he finished his work five years later and called it *A Compendium of the War of the Rebellion.* Dyer's work was reproduced in 1959 in three volumes by T. Y. Yoseloff, that untiring publisher of rare and out-of-print Civil War books, so it is readily available in every large library. There are other Union regimental compilations, such as the out-of-print *The Union Army,* published by the Federal Publishing Company, but none are as readily available as Dyer's *Compendium.*

Unfortunately, there is nothing from the South comparable to Dyer's *Compendium.* The closest thing to a single collection of Southern regimental histories is the twelve-volume *Confederate Military History,* edited by General C. A. Evans of Georgia and published in 1899. This book also has recently been reprinted by Yoseloff and is in most libraries. Some books in this set cover two states, some only a single state. The volumes are as follows, should you wish to order a particular state's history through interlibrary loan:

General history	Volume 1
Maryland and West Virginia	" 2
Virginia	" 3
North Carolina	" 4
South Carolina	" 5
Georgia	" 6
Alabama and Mississippi	" 7
Tennessee	" 8
Kentucky and Missouri	" 9
Louisiana and Arkansas	" 10
Texas and Florida	" 11
Index	" 12

A page from Dyer's three-volume Compendium of the War of the Rebellion. *In it Dyer, a Civil War veteran, compiled a short history of each Union regiment in the war. Unfortunately, no such volume exists for the regiments of the South.* ▶

North Anna River May 23-26. Line of the Pamunkey May 26-28. Totopotomoy May 28-31. Cold Harbor June 1-12. Before Petersburg June 16-19. Siege of Petersburg June 16, 1864, to April 2, 1865. Jerusalem Plank Road June 22-23, 1864. Deep Bottom, north of the James, July 27-28. Mine Explosion, Petersburg, July 30 (Reserve). Demonstration north of the James August 13-20. Strawberry Plains, Deep Bottom, August 14-18. Ream's Station August 25. Boydton Plank Road, Hatcher's Run. October 27-28. Dabney's Mills February 5-7, 1865. Appomattox Campaign March 28-April 9. Boydton Road March 30-31. Fall of Petersburg April 2. Sailor's Creek April 6. High Bridge April 6-7. Farmville April 7. Appomattox C. H. April 9. Surrender of Lee and his army. At Burkesville April 11-May 2. March to Washington, D. C., May 2-15. Grand Review May 23. Mustered out May 31 and discharged June 7, 1865. Recruits transferred to 1st Maine Heavy Artillery.

Regiment lost during service 3 Officers and 189 Enlisted men killed and mortally wounded and 2 Officers and 182 Enlisted men by disease. Total 376.

20th REGIMENT INFANTRY.

Organized at Portland and mustered in August 29, 1862. Left State for Alexandria, Va., September 3. Attached to 1st Brigade, 1st Division, 5th Army Corps, Army Potomac, to October, 1862. 3rd Brigade, 1st Division, 5th Army Corps, to July, 1865.

SERVICE.—Battle of Antietam, Md., September 16-17, 1862. Shephardstown September 19. Advance to Falmouth, Va., October-November. Battle of Fredericksburg, Va., December 12-15. Expedition to Richards and Ellis Fords December 20-30. "Mud March" January 20-24, 1863. Chancellorsville Campaign April 27-May 6. Battle of Chancellorsville May 1-5. Gettysburg (Pa.) Campaign June 12-July 24. Aldie June 17. Upperville and Upperville June 21. Middleburg June 24. Battle of Gettysburg July 1-3. Pursuit of Lee to Manassas Gap, Va., July 5-24. Bristoe Campaign October 9-22. Advance to line of the Rappahannock November 7-8. Rappahannock Station November 7. Mine Run Campaign November 26-December 2. Campaign from the Rapidan to the James May 3-June 15, 1864. Battles of the Wilderness May 5-7. Laurel Hill May 8. Spottsylvania May 8-12. Spottsylvania C. H. May 12-21. North Anna River May 23-26. Jericho Mills May 23. Line of the Pamunkey May 26-28. Totopotomoy May 28-31. Cold Harbor June 1-3. Bethesda Church June 1-3. Before Petersburg June 16-19. Siege of Petersburg June 16, 1864, to April 2, 1865. Weldon Railroad June 21-23, 1864. Mine Explosion, Petersburg, July 30 (Reserve). Six Mile House, Weldon Railroad, August 18-21. Poplar Springs Church, Peeble's Farm, September 29-October 2. Hatcher's Run October 27-28. Warren's Hicksford Raid December 7-11. Dabney's Mills, Hatcher's Run, February 5-7, 1865. Appomattox Campaign March 28-April 9. White Oak Road March 30. Quaker Road March 30. Boydton Road March 30-31. Five Forks April 1. Amelia C. H. April 5. High Bridge April 6. Appomattox C. H. April 9. Surrender of Lee and his army. March to Washington, D. C., May 2-12. Grand Review May 23. Mustered out—Old members, June 4; Regiment, July 16, 1865.

Regiment lost during service 9 Officers and 138 Enlisted men killed and mortally wounded and 1 Officer and 145 Enlisted men by disease. Total 293.

21st REGIMENT INFANTRY.

Organized at Augusta and mustered in for nine months' service October 14, 1862. Left State for Washington, D. C., October 21. Ordered on reaching Trenton, N. J., to return to New York, and duty at East New York till January, 1863. Embarked for New Orleans, La., January 9. Companies "A," "C," "E," "F," "H" and "K," on Steamer "Onward," reach New Orleans January 31, and moved to Baton Rouge, La., February 3. Balance of Regiment arrive at Baton Rouge February 11. Attached to 1st Brigade, 1st Division, 19th Army Corps, Dept. of the Gulf, to July, 1863.

SERVICE.—Operations against Port Hudson March 7-20, 1863. Duty at Baton Rouge till May. Advance on Port Hudson May 20-24. Action at Plains Store May 21. Siege of Port Hudson May 24-July 8. Assaults on Port Hudson May 27 and June 14. Surrender of Port Hudson July 8. Ordered home July 24. Mustered out August 25, 1863, expiration of term.

Regiment lost during service 1 Officer and 26 Enlisted men killed and mortally wounded and 1 Officer and 144 Enlisted men by disease. Total 172.

22nd REGIMENT INFANTRY.

Organized at Bangor and mustered in for nine months' service October 10, 1862. Left State for Washington, D. C., October 21. Duty at Arlington Heights, Va., till November 3. Moved to Fortress Monroe, Va., November 3, thence to Ship Island, Miss., and New Orleans, La., December 2-15. Attached to Grover's Division, Dept. of the Gulf, to January, 1863. 1st Brigade, 4th Division, 19th Army Corps, Army Gulf, to July, 1863.

SERVICE.—Moved to Baton Rouge, La., January 16, 1863. Duty there till March. Operations against Port Hudson, La., March 7-20. Moved to Donaldsonville March 26, thence to Brashear City. Operations in Western Louisiana April 9-May 14. Teche Campaign April 11-20. Porter's and McWilliams' Plantations at Indian Bend April 13. Irish Bend April 14. Moved to Franklin April 15. Bayou Vermillion April 17. Moved to New Iberia April 25; to Washington May 6, thence to Brashear City May 11-27. Moved to Port Hudson May 28. Siege of Port Hudson June 1-July 8. Assault at Port Hudson June 14. Surrender of Port Hudson July 8. Ordered home July 24. Mustered out August 14, 1863, expiration of term.

Regiment lost during service 1 Officer and 8 Enlisted men killed and mortally wounded and 2 Officers and 169 Enlisted men by disease. Total 180.

23rd REGIMENT INFANTRY.

Organized at Portland and mustered in for nine months' service September 29, 1862. Left State for Washington, D. C., October 18. Attached to Grover's Brigade, Defences of Washington, to February, 1863. Jewett's Brigade, 22nd Corps, to June, 1863. Slough's Brigade, Defences of Alexandria, 22nd Corps, to July, 1863.

SERVICE.—Camp at East Capital Hill till October 25, 1862. Moved to Seneca, Md., October 25, and guard duty along the Potomac River till April 19, 1863. Stationed at Edwards Ferry December, 1862, to April, 1863. Moved to Poolsville April 19, thence to Washington May 5, and to Alexandria May 24. Moved to Poolesville, Md., June 17, thence to Harper's Ferry, W. Va. Mustered out July 15, 1863, expiration of term.

Regiment lost during service 56 Enlisted men by disease.

24th REGIMENT INFANTRY.

Organized at Augusta and mustered in for nine months' service October 16, 1862. Left State for New York City October 29. Duty at East New York till January 12, 1863. Moved to Fortress Monroe, Va., thence to New Orleans, La., January 12-February 14. Attached to 3rd Brigade, 2nd Division, 19th Army Corps, Dept. of the Gulf, to July, 1863.

SERVICE.—Moved to Bonnet Carre, La., February 26, 1863, and duty there till May. Expedition to Ponchatoula and Amite River March 21-30. Capture of Ponchatoula March 24. Amite River March 28. Expedition to Amite River May 7-21. Civiques Ferry May 10. Advance on Port Hudson May 21-24. Siege of Port Hudson May 24-July 8. Assaults on Port Hudson, May 27 and June 14. Surrender of Port Hudson July 8. Ordered home July 24, and mustered out August 25, 1863, expiration of term.

Regiment lost during service 1 Enlisted man killed and 5 Officers and 185 Enlisted men by disease. Total 191.

These volumes vary in quality, for the state histories were written by different notable Confederates of varying historical competence and talent. Some of the histories, such as that of Florida, are well organized. Texas, in the same volume, is spotty and poorly done. At any rate, they may be of some help to you. For a starter, you should go to Volume 12, which contains the Index. As mentioned before, the greatest virtue of these books is that they are available almost anywhere in the United States, and they do cover many Southern regiments.

Most states that participated in the war also published their own official histories of each of their fighting units. Illinois has published eight volumes of regimental histories, *Report of the Adjutant General of the State of Illinois for the Years 1861–1866*; Massachusetts, *Massachusetts Soldiers, Sailors and Marines in the Civil War*, eight volumes; Florida, *Soldiers of Florida in the Seminole Indian, Civil and Spanish-American Wars*, one volume; New York, *New York in the War of the Rebellion, 1861–1865*, six volumes. A list of the most useful regimental histories according to the leading authorities of each state will be found in Appendix C. Additions to this list can be found in Dornbusch's general references for each state.

If you cannot locate your regiment, use Dyer or the *OR* to see with whom your regiment was brigaded. It was a Civil War practice to band three to five regiments together into a brigade in which they fought as a unit. Thus the story of your brigade is essentially the story of your regiment. A trace of the other regiments in that brigade may lead directly to references to actions of your own regiment and enable you to begin putting the pieces together.

The biggest drawback to the state histories is usually their unavailability outside the individual states. Very few have been reprinted in modern times, and sometimes you cannot get them through interlibrary loan because they are too valuable to lend indiscriminately. You can have a distant library Xerox a particular regimental history. You may want to get an estimate of the cost for reproducing a page, for the total bill may run to more than you will want to pay for reproduction.

In addition to the official state regimental histories, which often are very brief, there are hundreds upon hundreds of single volumes devoted to one and only one regiment. The best of these will give you really splendid word pictures of marches, battle scenes, and descriptions of officers, messmates, and friends of your soldier, or of your soldier himself. In quite a few there are photographs of members of the regiment. Almost always there are a few pictures of the leading regimental officers and in many cases photographs of enlisted men. It is here that you may find a picture of great-grandfather or a photograph to go with your inscribed sword.

As for Civil War pictures in general, the best and most complete set can be found in *The Photographic History of the Civil War,* in ten volumes, edited by Francis T. Miller and published in 1912 by the Review of Reviews Company. This work has been republished recently in five volumes by Yoseloff.

At the beginning of the war, Matthew B. Brady, the wealthiest and most-noted photographer in America, went off to war. With his great wooden box cameras, glass plates, chemicals, and trained assistants, he followed the Union army from one bloody battlefield to another. Four years and thousands of photographs later, Brady returned to his Washington and New York studios, bankrupt. He never recovered financially from the effects of the war and died in obscurity at seventy-three in Washington, D.C., in 1896. It is Brady's photographs, taken during his four-year stay with the Federal army, that fill the ten volumes of Miller's *Photographic History of the Civil War.* You will probably not find your great-grandfather's picture here. You will find in these ten volumes, however, the finest and most complete set of battlefield photographs, portraits, camp and on-the-march pictures in existence. This is the ultimate source for all Civil War pictorial history. The photographic works of Alexander Gardner, one of Brady's assistants, were printed by Philip and Solomons in 1865 and reprinted by Dover Press in 1959 in a book entitled *Gardner's Photographic Sketch Book of the War*. Most of these pictures are included in Miller's ten volumes.

A few days after a bullet from John Wilkes Booth's tiny derringer pistol had smashed into the back of Abraham Lincoln's head, a small body of Union army and navy officers banded together in Philadelphia to act as a guard of honor to the president's body as it lay in state. After the war these men organized the first Civil War veterans' organization, the "Military Order of Loyal Legions of the United States." "Commanderies" were formed in a number of northern and western states. Sixteen of these commanderies—Indiana, Illinois, Iowa, Kansas, Maine, Massachusetts, Michigan, Minnesota, Missouri, Nebraska, New York, Ohio, Oregon, Pennsylvania, Wisconsin, and the District of Columbia —published numerous books containing rosters, war papers, personal reminiscences, Civil War sketches and incidents. The quality of these commandery publications varies. They are about Northern soldiers only, and the books are seldom found outside the state in which the commandery originated. When you are at a dead end, MOLLUS, the abbreviation scholars give to this organization, may help. Some states will send out their MOLLUS copies on interlibrary loan; others keep them under lock and key but will Xerox or otherwise duplicate them for you for a small fee. Strange to say, the largest and most important of all Union veterans' organizations, "The Grand Army of the Republic," known as the GAR, published practically nothing.

There are several other Civil War publications that may help you in a search for veterans' pictures and stories. *The Confederate Veteran* is the best publication concerning the Southern soldier. It was published monthly in Nashville, Tennessee, from 1893 to 1932. This set of magazines contains one of the largest collections of Confederate memoirs, anecdotes, incidents, and personal stories in existence. Along with the stories are thousands of postwar photographs of veterans, reunion pictures, and memorial photographs of deceased veterans taken right up to the great depression of the 1930's. At the end of each year's series of magazines there is an index. There áre forty volumes in all. For researchers who find that they are using this set of magazines quite often, all forty indexes have been collected into one volume entitled *The Confederate Veteran Magazine Index*. It is published by the Morningside Bookshop, P. O. Box 336, Forest Park Station, Dayton, Ohio 45405.

Before leaving *The Confederate Veteran*, remember that its photographs of Southern veterans are unsurpassed. Your ancestor may well be here, and the notice of his death will in all probability be here, even if there is no picture.

A modern magazine in which you will often turn up photographs not found in Miller's set is *Civil War Times Illustrated*.

The best nonphotographic works are Frank Leslie's *Illustrated History of the Civil War,* now long out of print, and *Harper's Weekly*. The wartime pictures of *Harper's Weekly* have recently (1960) been reprinted in four volumes by Living History, Inc., Box 130, Shenandoah, Iowa 51601. Unfortunately, the nonphotographic books will be of little use to you as a researcher. This is because very few soldiers had their portraits sketched by war correspondents or artists, and most of the battle scenes and camp-life drawings of the war contain more artistic fancy than fact.

6 / Personnel Files and Rosters

Personnel files, as mentioned earlier, are records that have to do with a soldier's leaves, promotions, illnesses, special assignments, and so on. The personnel records in the National Archives are all based on documents collected by the federal government. Often you will find that these records are not complete. Many times they may give only an enlistment date or the number of a regiment. It is not unusual for the National Archives to have nothing at all on your man. In any case, you should turn to the ever-helpful Dornbusch and to Nevins, Robertson, and Wiley to locate books containing personnel files and rosters. These are the files and rosters that most state archives and other institutions must turn to in order to send you personnel data when you request it from them. You can save some time by doing it yourself if a good library is available.

After you have traced six or eight soldiers, you will become aware that your most successful hunts were for Civil War officers. One of the very best publications of officer biographies happened to appear in a paperback edition just after the war. Published by the United States Adjutant General's Office in eight volumes, it was entitled *Official Army Register of the Volunteer Force of the United States Army for the Years 1861, 1862, 1863, 1864, 1865.* These volumes list only the volunteer officers who served in the million-and-a-half-man Union volunteer army. The contents of the volumes are as follows:

Volume 1 New England
"   2 New York, New Jersey
"   3 Pennsylvania, Delaware, Maryland, District of Columbia
"   4 West Virginia, Virginia, North Carolina, South Carolina, Georgia, Florida, Alabama, Mississippi,

> Tennessee, Louisiana, Kentucky, Texas, Arkansas
> "   5   Ohio, Michigan
> "   6   Indiana, Illinois
> "   7   Missouri, Wisconsin, Iowa, Minnesota, California, Oregon, Nevada
> "   8   The territories of Washington, New Mexico, Nebraska, Colorado, Dakota
>   Special Troops: Veterans Reserve Corps, United States Veteran Volunteers, United States Volunteers, United States Colored Troops

In addition to the above set, the Adjutant General's Office also published seven more volumes entitled *Official Army Register for 1861–1865*. Here you will find biographies of all the regular officers in the Federal army during the war. Outstanding as both these sets are, they are, nevertheless, a bit hard to locate, and only the largest libraries will have them. If you are unable to locate copies anywhere else, the United States Adjutant General's Office has them, and a letter to it may find your officer in blue. Address your letter to

> United States Adjutant General's Office
> The Pentagon
> Washington, D.C. 20310

Another reference tool is Francis B. Heitman's collection of biographical sketches of all the regular army officers entitled *Historical Register and Dictionary of the United States Army, from Its Organization, September 29, 1789, to March 2, 1903*. The University of Illinois Press has reprinted it, so the book is easily available. Not only is Heitman a quick reference, but it could be useful in a very difficult situation. Suppose you have a photograph of a Union officer and on the back is "Captain Sam Jones" and nothing else. Cross your fingers and open up Heitman. If Captain Jones was in the regular army, Heitman will give you a summary of his service. It may be just the lead you will need.

In 1880 Thomas H. S. Hamersly edited and published the *Complete Regular Army Register of the United States: For 100 Years (1779–1879)*. This volume is similar to Heitman's but not nearly so complete. In 1892 and 1893 Lieutenant Colonel William H. Powell of the United States Army published *Officers of the Army and Navy (Regular) Who Served in the Civil War* and a companion volume, *Officers of the Army and Navy (Volunteer) Who Served in the Civil War*. This latter volume is much used by Civil War buffs. Both these books were published by the L. R. Hamersly Company of Philadelphia. For this reason, they are commonly called "Hamersly's" instead of "Powell's" volumes, as they should be.

Similar to Powell's publication is General George W. Cullum's two-volume *Biographical Register of the Officers and Graduates of the United States Military Academy at West Point, New York, from Its Establishment, March 16, 1802, to the Reorganization of 1866–67*. Though no longer in print, it is available in larger libraries and is the best there is on West Pointers.

Lewis Hamersly enters the picture again, not as Powell's publisher, but as the author of his own book, *The Records of Living Officers of the United States Navy and Marine Corps*, Philadelphia, 1870. Here you will find short biographies of United States naval officers from first lieutenant up who survived the battles of the Union navy during the war and were still alive in 1870.

For Rebel naval officers the best source is a volume first published by the United States Naval Records Office and republished in 1931: *Officers in the Confederate States Navy, 1861–65*. This work is not often found on the average library shelf. It is available through interlibrary loan, of course. There is also a listing

---

A page from Francis B. Heitman's Historical Register and Dictionary of the United States Army. *It lists short biographies of all regular United States Army officers who served from 1789 to 1903. There are other books that list state volunteer officers as well.* See page 59.

▶

Cushing, John W. N H. 2 lt 45 inf 21 Apr 1814; 1 lt 1 Sept 1814; resd 7 Jan 1815; [died 3 Mar 1836.]

*****Cushing, Samuel Tobey.** R I. R I. Cadet M A 1 July 1855 (**30**); bvt 2 lt 10 inf 1 July 1860; 2 lt 2 inf 19 Jan 1861; 1 lt 14 May 1861; capt 15 Feb 1862; capt c s 9 Feb 1863; maj c s 28 Aug 1888; lt col a c g s 11 Nov 1895; col a c g s 26 Jan 1897; brig gen comsy gen 28 Jan 1898; bvt maj 13 Mar 1865 for fai and mer ser dur the war; retd 21 Apr 1898; died 21 July 1901.

*****Cushing, Thomas Humphrey.** Mass. Mass. Sergt 6 contl inf Jan to Dec 1776; 2 lt 1 Mass 1 Jan 1777; 1 lt 12 Jan 1778; taken prisoner at —— 14 May 1781; exchanged ——; bvt capt 30 Sept 1783; retained in Jackson's contl regt Nov 1783 and served to 20 June 1784; capt 2 inf 4 Mar 1791; assd to 2 sublegion 4 Sept 1792; maj 1 sublegion 3 Mar 1793; inspr the Army 27 Feb 1797 to 22 May 1798; lt col 2 inf 1 Apr 1802; adjt and I G 26 Mar 1802 to 9 May 1807; col 2 inf 7 Sept 1805; brig gen 2 July 1812; hon dischd 15 June 1815; [died 19 Oct 1822.]

Cushman, Alden G. Mass. 1 lt 4 inf 3 May 1808; dismd 3 July 1809.

Cushman, Allerton Seward. Italy. Mass. Pvt A 6 Mass inf 12 May to 1 Sept 1898; capt c s vols 11 Aug 1898; hon dischd 31 Dec 1898.

Cushman, C. Seth. Me. Wis. 1 lt 14 inf 5 Aug 1861; r adjt 15 Oct 1863 to 6 Dec 1864; resd 6 Dec 1864; [died 9 Jan 1883.]

Cushman, Caleb. Army. Sergt 9 inf 25 June 1812 to Mar 1814; ens 9 inf 30 Mar 1814; 3 lt 1 May 1814; 2 lt 25 July 1814; r adjt Aug 1814 to June 1815; 1 lt 31 Oct 1814; hon dischd 15 June 1815.

Cushman, Charles. Mass. Ens 34 inf 26 July 1814; 3 lt 1 Oct 1814; 2 lt 1 Jan 1815; hon dischd 15 June 1815.

Cushman, Eugene. Pa. Pa. 2 lt 16 inf 17 Dec 1872; 1 lt 15 Mar 1883; resd 1 Oct 1888.

Cushman, Guy. R I. Mo. Pvt and corpl M 1 Mo inf 14 May 1898; tr to D 1 Ohio cav 16 July 1898; hon must out 23 Oct 1898; 2 lt inf 10 Apr 1899; tr to 2 cav 10 May 1899; 1 lt 11 cav 2 Feb 1901.

Cushman, Herbert. Pa. Pa. Cadet naval academy 23 Sept 1862 to 8 Apr 1864; 2 lt 20 inf 23 June 1868; 1 lt 22 Oct 1876; retd 27 Apr 1891.

Cusick, Cornelius Charles. N Y. N Y. 2 lt 132 N Y inf 14 Aug 1862; 1 lt 1 July 1863; hon must out 29 June 1865; 2 lt 13 inf 20 June 1866; tr to 31 inf 21 Sept 1866; tr to 22 inf 15 May 1869; 1 lt 5 Aug 1872; capt 1 Jan 1888; retd 14 Jan 1892.

Custer, Bethel Moore. Pa. Pa. Pvt C 19 Pa inf 18 Apr to 9 Aug 1861; corpl and sergt C 90 Pa inf 17 Sept 1861 to 27 Feb 1864; 2 lt 32 U S c inf 4 Mar 1864; 1 lt 26 Nov 1864; hon must out 22 Aug 1865; 1 lt 11 U S c inf 22 Oct 1865; hon must out 12 Jan 1866; 2 lt 38 inf 28 July 1866; tr to 24 inf 11 Nov 1869; 1 lt 1 Mar 1871; r q m 15 May 1877 to 30 Apr 1880; capt 18 June 1880; bvt 1 lt 2 Mar 1867 for gal and mer ser at James Island S C; died 22 Dec 1887.

*****Custer, George Armstrong.** Ohio. Ohio. Cadet M A 1 July 1857 (**34**); 2 lt 2 cav 24 June 1861; 5 cav 3 Aug 1861; 1 lt 17 July 1862; capt a a d c 5 June 1862; hon dischd as a a d c 31 Mar 1863; brig gen vols 29 June 1863; maj gen vols 15 Apr 1865; hon must out of vol ser 1 Feb 1866; capt 5 cav 8 May 1864; lt col 7 cav 28 July 1866; bvt maj 3 July 1863 for gal and mer ser in the battle of Gettysburg Pa; lt col 11 May 1864 for gal and mer ser in the battle of Yellow Tavern Va; col 19 Sept 1864 for gal and mer ser in the battle of Winchester Va; brig gen 13 Mar 1865 for gal and mer ser in the battle of Five Forks Va; maj gen 13 Mar 1865 for gal and mer ser dur the campn ending in the surrender of the insurgent army of northern Va and maj gen vols 19 Oct 1864 for gal and mer ser at the battles of Winchester and Fishers Hill Va; killed 25 June 1876 and his whole command massacred in action with Sioux Inds at Little Big Horn river Mont.

Custer, Thomas Ward. Ohio. Mich. Pvt H 21 Ohio inf 2 Sept 1861 to 10 Oct 1864; 2 lt 6 Mich cav 8 Nov 1864; bvt 1 lt capt and maj vols 13 Mar 1865 for dist and gal con; hon must out 24 Nov 1865; 2 lt 1 inf 23 Feb 1866; 1 lt 7 cav 28 July 1866; r q m 3 Dec 1866 to 10 Mar 1867; capt 2 Dec 1875; bvt capt 2 Mar 1867 for gal and dist con in the engagement with the enemy at Waynesboro Va 2 Mar 1865; maj 2 Mar 1867 for dist con in the engagement with the enemy at Namozine Church Va 3 Apr 1865 and lt col 2 Mar 1867 for dist courage and ser at the battle of Sailors Creek Va; awarded medal of honor 24 Apr 1865 for the capture of a flag at Nanzomine Church Va 2 Apr 1865 and another medal of honor 22 May 1865 for the capture of a flag at Sailors Creek Va 6 Apr 1865; killed 25 June 1876 in action with Sioux Inds at Little Big Horn river Mont.

Custis, George Washington Parke. Md. Va. Cor lht drgs 8 Jan 1799; 2 lt 3 Mar 1799; hon dischd 15 June 1800; [died 10 Oct 1857.]

Custis, Lebbeus. Army. Sergt maj 3 art; 2 lt 3 art 1 Oct 1813; resd 7 Feb 1814.

of Confederate naval and marine officers as of January 1, 1864, in Vol. XII, pp. 110–19 of C. A. Evans' *Confederate Military History* (see page 52). Here you will find only name and rank, however.

Chasing your army officer down another avenue, you can try the general state regimental collections. As mentioned earlier, most states have one or a series of books outlining histories of each and every military unit called into state service. Included either in these histories or in separate books are rosters of every soldier and sailor who ever served in any of the state's regiments, naval units, and so forth. These pages and pages of lists of soldiers usually give brief summaries of the service of each man. Many of these rosters will be useful to you if you are at the beginning of your search, for they will give you data on your soldier's regiment, company, enlistment, and termination of service. This information can be readily supplied by the state archives (see Chapter III), but you will have to wait. On the other hand, a quick trip to the library may get you the information in an hour instead of a few weeks. A disadvantage of these rosters is that they, like the regimental histories, are seldom found outside their particular states.

Some of these rosters are huge sets. North Carolina is in the process of compiling twelve volumes entitled *North Carolina Troops, 1861–1865: A Roster*. Here are all the names of her servicemen, officers and enlisted men combined. Massachusetts has nine volumes, *Massachusetts Soldiers, Sailors and Marines in the Civil War*; Pennsylvania, five volumes. Michigan has its forty-six-volume *Record of Service of Michigan Volunteers in the Civil War, 1861–1865*; and Louisiana's three volumes are called *Records of Louisiana Confederate Soldiers and Louisiana Confed-*

A typical page of a state veterans' roster. This one was organized in three volumes by Andrew B. Booth and is a standard reference for Louisiana troops. It includes all soldiers from privates to generals. See Appendix C for comparable volumes in your state. ▶

1863. Forwd. from Old Capitol Prison, Washington, D. C., to Fort Delaware, Del., May 7th, 1863. Paroled at Fort Delaware, Del. Exchanged at City Pt., Va., May 23rd, 1863. Rolls from May, 1863, to Feb., 1864, Present. Federal Rolls of Prisoners of War, Captured Spottsylvania C. H., May 12th, 1864. Recd. at Pt. Lookout, Md., from Belle Plains, Va., May 18th, 1864. Forwd. to Elmira, N. Y., Aug. 17th, 1864. Paroled at Elmira, N. Y., Oct. 11th, 1864. Died at Fort Monroe, Va., Nov. 5th, 1864.

Davis, Edward, Pvt. Co. C. 5th La. Infty. En. May 19th, 1861, Camp Moore. La. Apptd. 3rd Corpl. Aug. 18th, 1861; 6th Segt., Oct. 5th, 1861. Present on all Rolls to Oct., 1862. Rolls Nov. 1862, to April, 1864, Detached on Division Pioneer Corps. Roll April to Aug., 1864, dated Nov., 1864, Present. Born in New York, occupation caulker, single, Res. New Orleans, La.

Davis, Edward, Pvt. Co. A. 1st La. Hvy. Arty. (Regulars). En. May 5th, 1864, Oxford, Miss. Roll for March and April, 1865, Deserted from near Cuba Station April 25th. Appears on Roll, not dated, of Prisoners of War. Surrendered at Post of La Grange, Tenn., May 17th, 1865. Remarks: Left his command at Cuba, Ala., May 1st, 1865. Paroled.

Davis, Elisha W., Pvt. Co. A. 28th (Gray's) La. Infty. En. May 14th, 1862, Monroe, La. Roll for July and Aug., 1863, Detached as Nurse at Hospl., Shreveport, La., from May 15th.

Davis, F. M., Pvt. Co. D. 4th La. Cav. On Roll of Prisoners of War. Paroled at Monroe, La., June 17th, 1865. Res. Union Par., La.

Davis, Fletcher W., Pvt. Co. I. 9th La. Infty. En. Franklinton, La., April 17th, 1862. Record copied from Memorial Hall, New Orleans, La., by the War Dept., Washington, D. C., June, 1903, Born Louisiana, occupation farmer, age when enlisted 16, single, Res. Franklinton, La. Died Charlottesville, Va., May 30th, 1862.

Davis, Florian, Pvt. Co. C. 21st (Patton's) La. Infty. En. Dec. 4th, 1862, Camp Moore, La. Present on Rolls to Feb., 1863. Rolls from Sept., 1863, to Dec., 1863, Absent without leave since Aug. 23rd, 1863. Federal Rolls of Prisoners of War, Captured Vicksburg, Miss., July 4th, 1863. Paroled at Marine Hospl., Vicksburg, Miss., July 17th, 1863.

Davis, Florian, Capt. Co. H. 4th Regt. 1st Brig. 1st Div. La. Militia. On Roll not dated, ordered into service of the State of Louisiana.

Davis, Francois, Pvt. Co. H. 1st La. Hvy. Arty. (Regulars). En. Aug. 6th, 1862, ——. Roll for Nov. and Dec., 1862, Died in Hospl., Dec. 8th, 1862. (Substitute.)

Davis, Francis M., Pvt. Co. E. 12th La. Infty. En. Aug. 18th, 1861, Camp Moore, La. Present to Oct. 31st, 1861. Roll dated June 30th, 1862, Absent. Detailed on guard duty on the railroad above Grenada, Miss., by order Col. Scott, June 16th, 1862.

Davis, Frank A., Pvt. Sergt. Co. F. 3rd La. Infty. En. May 17th, 1861, New Orleans, La. Present on Roll to June 30th, 1861. Roll for July and Aug., 1861, Absent. Nurse at Springfield, Mo. Rolls from Sept., 1861, to April, 1862, Present. Roll for May and June, 1862, Present. Promoted 2nd Corpl. May 16th, 1862. Rolls from July, 1862, to Oct., 1862, Present. Roll for Nov. and Dec., 1862, Resigned as Corpl., Nov. 18th, 1862. Federal Rolls of Prisoners of War, Captured Vicksburg, Miss., July 4th, 1863. Paroled at Vicksburg, July 8th, 1863. Reported in camp for exchange at Natchitoches, La., April 1st, 1864. Rolls of Prisoners of War, Paroled Shreveport, La., June 7th, 1865. Res. Shreveport, La.

Davis, Frank R., Pvt. Co. C. 1st (Nelligan's) La. Infty. En. May 27th, 1861, New Orleans, La. Present on all Rolls to Dec., 1861. Roll Jan. and Feb., 1862, Absent. Guard House. Roll March and April 1862, Present. Rolls June, 1862, to Oct. 31st, 1862, Killed in action June 25th, 1862, near Seven Pines.

Davis, G., Pvt. Cage's La. Cav. Co. F. Federal Rolls of Prisoners of War, Captured East Baton Rouge, La., Jan. 16th, 1865. Transfd. to Vicksburg, Miss., May 11th, 1865, from New Orleans, La.

Davis, G. L., Pvt. Co. D. 25th La. Infty. Roll for March 6th, 1862, to ——, 186—, dated March 26th, —— (only Roll on file). En. March 6th, 1862, Morehouse Par., La. Entitled to bounty of fifty dollars.

Davis, G. L. C., Pvt. Powers Regt. ——. Federal Rolls of Prisoners of War, Captured Warrington Co., Miss., Nov. 11th, 1865. Paroled in New Orleans, La., in Military Prison, June 3rd, 1865.

Davis, G. L. C., Pvt. Continental Regt. La. Militia. Roll dated New Orleans, La., Nov. 23rd, 1861, shows him on parade.

Davis, G. L. C., Jr., Pvt. Co. E. Crescent Regt. La. Infty. En. March 5th, 1862, New Orleans, La. Roll for May and June, 1862, Absent. Sick.

Davis, G. M., Pvt. Co. H. 6th La. Cav. On Roll of Prisoners of War, Paroled at Natchitoches, La., June 26th, 1865. Res. Bienville Par., La.

Davis, G. P., Sergt. Co. D. Perkins Battn. Rolls of Prisoners of War, Paroled at Shreveport, La., June 7th, 1865. Res. Denton Co., Tex.

Davis, G. W., Sergt. Co. H. 8h La. Cav. On Roll of Prisoners of War, Paroled Shreveport, La., June 21st, 1865. Res. Bossier Par., La.

Davis, George, Pvt. Doyle's Co. Ogden's La. Cav. On Roll of Prisoners of War, not dated, Captured near East Baton Rouge, La., Jan. 17th, 1865. Transfd. to New Orleans, La., Jan. 31st, 1865.

Davis, George, Pvt. Corpl. Co. G. 5th La. Infty. En. May 20th, 1861, New Orleans, La., age 40 years. Present on all Rolls to Aug., 1862, Sept. and Oct., 1862, Absent. Appointed Oct. 1st, 1862, 2nd Corpl. Sick in Winchester. Nov. and Dec., 1862, Present. Jan. and Feb., 1863, Absent on 30 days' furlough from Feb. 19th, 1863. Roll March and April, 1863, Died at Hospl. in Lynchburg, Va. Born in Ireland, occupation laborer, age when enlisted 32, single, Res. St. Louis, Mo.

Davis, George, 8th La. Infty. Appears on Federal Register of Prisoners, Confined in Guard House, Fort Monroe, Va., June 24th, 1864. Sent to Military Prison, Camp Hamilton, Va., July 1st, 1864. Sent to New York, via Baltimore, July 10th, 1864.

Davis, George, Pvt. Co. I. 15th La. Infty. En. June 9th, 1861, Camp Moore, La. Appears on Report of Deaths, remark: Died Sept. 1861, at Centerville, Va., of typhoid fever. Born in Louisiana, occupation farmer, age when enlisted 26, single, Res. Trinity, La.

Davis, George, Pvt. Co. —— Miles Legion La. Militia. On Rolls of Prisoners of War, Captured at East Baton Rouge, La., Jan. 16th, 1865. Sent to New Orleans, La., Jan. 22nd, 1865. Exchanged May 11th, 1865.

Davis, George W., Pvt. Old Co. D. 1st Spec. Battn. (Wheat's) La. Infty. En. June 8th, 1861, Camp Moore, La. On Roll to Aug. 3rd., 1861, Present or absent not stated.

Davis, Ghershom S., Musician Pvt. Cos. K. F. and G. 31st La. Infty. En. Jan. 27th, 1863, Monroe, La. Roll for Jan. and Feb., 1863, Present. Apptd. Chf. Musician, order of Col. C. H. Morrison, Jan. 27th, 1863. Federal Rolls of Prisoners of War show him captured and paroled at Vicksburg, Miss., July 4th, 1863. Paroled at Monroe, La., June 6th, 1865. Res. Oachita Par., La.

Davis, H. H., Sergt. Co. —— Ogden's La. Cav. Federal Rolls of Prisoners of War show

erate Commands. Appendix C lists the regimental histories and rosters that are, according to the authorities of each state, the most useful.

Once you have obtained all the information you can from the state and national archives and have combed your available libraries for rosters and regimental histories, you will find still more doors to open. There are well over a thousand public and private museums, historical societies, and similar places where millions upon millions of individual items, diaries, letters, and the like, are kept. Some of these may play an important part in your search.

Each state has at least one, and often two, state historical societies that publish journals and have special archives. In addition, there are county, regional, city, and religious historical societies. Then there are special organizations such as the United Daughters of the Confederacy, the Association for the Preservation of Tennessee Antiquities, the Great Plains Historical Association, the Historic Mobile Preservation Society, the Dig and Delve Society (Indiana), and the Association for the Preservation of Virginia Antiquities. The list goes on and on. Most societies have special libraries, many publish documents, and most have special unpublished archives, which could very well be helpful to you in your quest.

Your guide to the historical societies and agencies is the *Directory of Historical Societies and Agencies in the United States and Canada,* published by the American Association for State and Local History, 132 Ninth Avenue North, Nashville, Tennessee 37203. Most libraries have a copy of this very useful book, but you may buy your own copy by writing to Nashville.

Last, there are countless museums with their historical treasures. There is no telling what might lie in one of these repositories. To give you some idea of the extent of the various holdings, if you were to eliminate the millions of books that are available in these special institutions, there would still remain on their shelves well over one hundred million separate historical items covering over three hundred years of American history.

Without some guide similar to Dornbusch to lead helpless laymen through the libraries, these sources would be useful to very few. In this case the hero who will come to your rescue is the late Philip Hamer, who compiled *A Guide to Archives and Manuscripts in the United States,* Yale University Press, New Haven, 1961. Hamer has listed, state by state and page by page, not only the location of every archive collection, but what it holds by title and subject, giving a brief description of each. His compilation, available in most libraries, is a truly wonderful book and is your most complete and convenient single-volume guide to all the special collections in the country. Of even greater value in searching for manuscripts is the multi-volumed *National Union Catalog of Manuscript Collections* published by the federal government and kept up to date by them. Because of their cost, these volumes are found only in the larger libraries. If you happen to have any idea of publishing or otherwise publicly presenting your findings on a soldier, sailor, or marine, you really must check Hamer and the *Union Catalog.* These books may tell you if you are about to leave out some useful, and perhaps vital, information. It has even made the difference between the success or failure of professional historians. Think what it could do for you!

Two guides similar to Hamer, but not nearly so complete, are the volumes mentioned in Chapter II: Munden and Beers' *Guide to Federal Archives Relating to the Civil War* and Beers' *Guide to the Archives of the Government of the Confederate States of*

On the following pages are but two of Philip Hamer's thousands of descriptions of materials held in public and private archives, museums, and libraries across the country. His book, A Guide to ▶ Archives and Manuscripts in the United States, *is necessary for a detailed search.*

17 items); Lyle Saxon (La.; author),
1929-45 (3,297 items); Ruth McEnery
Stuart (La.; short-story writer), 1879-
1912 (90 items); Ellsworth Woodward
(La.; artist), 1914-39 (528 items); and
William Woodward (La., Miss.; artist,
prof. of architecture at Tulane Univ.),
1893-1901 (280 items).

Other personal papers include
those of the Favrot family, chiefly
1750-1825 (2,000 items), and of several other distinguished Louisiana
families, 1710-1945. There are also
papers of several Louisiana plantation
owners, mostly for the pre-Civil War
period, and of a few New Orleans mer-
chants. Small groups of papers include
those of a physician, a ship chandler,
an engineer, several lawyers, and numerous other persons.

Also included are a collection of
maps of New Orleans and other parts
of Louisiana, 1608-1938 (749 items);
official records of New Orleans, 1770-
1893 (85 vols. and 1,177 items); records of the Poydraw Home (for or-
phans), 1817-1943 (10,000 pieces); and
records of a few churches, 1805-1900
(3 vols.). Records relating to science
and art include those of the Louisiana
section of the American Chemical Society, 1906-50 (24 vols. and 580
items); L'Athenée Louisianais, 1876-
86 (215 items); the New Orleans Academy of Sciences, 1858-1949 (252
items); the New Orleans Botanical Society, 1932-41 (1,040 items); and the
Southern States Art League, 1921-47
(907 items). There are also records
of two New Orleans banks, 1827-1903
(166 vols. and 1,114 items); and of the
Street and Electric Railway Union,
1902-40 (39 vols. and 6,961 items).
World War II letters, 1941-45, number 253.

The Louisiana Historical Association Collection, which is on permanent
deposit in the Library's Archives Department, is separately described below under the name of the Association.
See Hist. Records Survey, Guide

for La., pp. 14-16; and De Ricci,
Census, p. 741.

NEW ORLEANS 12

Louisiana Historical Association.
Confederate Memorial Hall, 929
Camp St. Kenneth Trist Urquhart,
Executive Secretary.

Holdings: 150,000 items, 1753-
1920 but primarily 1861-65, relating
chiefly to the Confederate States of
America and the Confederate Army
in the Civil War. Among the records
dated before the Civil War are papers
on the New Orleans campaign, 1814-
15 (554 pieces), including many
morning reports of units of the U.S.
Army and the Tennessee militia; and
papers of Albert Sidney Johnston
(Tex.; U.S. and Confed. Army officer) as U.S. Army paymaster at Austin, Tex., 1848-56 (3,651 pieces). Papers of Jefferson Davis (Miss.; U.S.
Rep. and Sen., Sec. War, Confed.
Pres.), 1845-91 (4,270 pieces), con-
stitute a major group and include
many official documents issued by
Davis as Confederate President.
There are also records of and relating to the executive departments of
the Confederate States, 1861-65 (1,152
pieces); the Confederate Adjutant and
Inspector General's Office (3,702
pieces); the Confederate Navy and Marine Corps (2,725 pieces); several military departments and districts of the
Confederacy (11,356 pieces); Confederate armies and troop units other
than Louisiana units (1,700 pieces);
and Louisiana units in Confederate
service (7,025 pieces). Included also
are manuscripts relating to Civil War
battles (2,000 pieces); maps, plans,
drawings, and plates of uniforms
(500 pieces); miscellaneous account
books, diaries, and reminiscences
from the Civil War period, and papers of Confederate veterans' orga-

nizations, including the associations of veterans of the Army of Northern Virginia and the Army of Tennessee. (All of the materials described in this entry, while still the property of the Association, are housed in the Archives Department, Howard-Tilton Memorial Library, Tulane University.)

See Hist. Records Survey, Guide for La., p. 4.

—oOo—

Louisiana Historical Society, 521 Carondelet Bldg.

Holdings: Included are transcripts of records in French archives relating to colonial Louisiana, 1678-1769, and to the transfer of Louisiana to the United States, 1803.

See Hist. Records Survey, Guide for La., p. 5; Roscoe R. Hill, American Missions in European Archives (1951), p. 110; and John S. Kendall, "Historical Collections in New Orleans," in N. C. Hist. Review, 7:463-476 (Oct. 1930).

NEW ORLEANS 16

Louisiana State Museum. 709 Chartres St.

Holdings: 400,000 pieces, relating chiefly to colonial Louisiana and to Confederate military history. Included are records of the Superior Council of Louisiana, 1717-69; judicial records of Spanish Louisiana, 1769-1803; some papers dealing with the Battle of New Orleans, 1815; and a large quantity of Confederate military records. Also included are papers of Daniel Clark (La.; Delegate to Cong. from the Terr. of Orleans, merchant); and 5 Civil War dispatch books of Richard Taylor (La.; Confed. Army officer).

See Hist. Records Survey, Guide for La., pp. 6-8; and John S. Kendall,

"Historical Collections in New Orleans," in N. C. Hist. Review, 7:463-476 (Oct. 1930).

NEW ORLEANS 18

Middle American Research Institute Library, Tulane University. Edith B. Ricketson, Institute Librarian.

Holdings: 108 linear ft. and 142 cu. ft., 1348-1960, relating chiefly to Mexico, Central America, and the West Indies. Included are the C. I. Fayssoux Collection of papers of William Walker (La., Calif.; leader of filibustering expeditions to Nicaragua), 1857-80 (551 pieces); a collection of Yucatecan letters, 1778-1863 (856 pieces); treatises on Middle American languages; and extensive government archives, especially for Guatemala.

See Hist. Records Survey, Guide for La., pp. 16-18, its Calendar of the Fayssoux Collection of William Walker Papers (1937. 28 p. Processed), and its Calendar of the Yucatecan Letters (1939. 240 p. Processed); and Marie Hunter Irvine, "Administrative Papers: Copies Relating to New Spain," in the Institute's Miscellaneous Series, No. 5 (1948. 28 p.).

NEW ORLEANS

Newmark Library. 836 Cambronne St.

Holdings: 737 pieces and 1 bundle, 1926-37, consisting of a collection pertaining to the American Old Catholic Church movement in the United States and Canada.

See Hist. Records Survey, Guide for La., p. 11.

America. Though these two books are primarily for government archives, they do mention quite a few nongovernment organizations and their holdings. The occasional Civil War searcher will find these books useful, and the professional will find them indispensable.

For those of you who wish to conduct a search on a local level beyond Hamer, there is an endless variety of Civil War related material in town halls, county courthouses, churches, and the like. If you live near the home town of your soldier, a local search is a must. Visit your town or county officials, your local reference librarian, and the nearest historical society leader. If they do not know what is available, then the records must have gone up in smoke in the last courthouse fire or been washed away in some spring flood. Then, too, not all towns or counties cared about their past, so they never bothered to collect or recollect. If you do not know the name of the library near your search area, simply go to the nearest library, which will doubtless have a copy of *The American Library Directory,* where you can get the address of any library in the country.

If, for some reason, you cannot visit the location that you wish, and overworked officials have no time to carry on a correspondence, there are usually professional genealogists and researchers who for a fee will do your research for you. For more information concerning genealogists, you may wish to write to the National Genealogical Society, 1921 Sunderland Place, N.W., Washington, D.C. 20036.

7 / Acquiring and Identifying Civil War Equipment

By now, you have seen how sources such as rosters, personnel files, and official records give the basic facts of a soldier's record. You have also learned how regimental histories, published personal memoirs and biographies, together with pictures and sketches, give life to your soldier and help fill in the blanks left by the official records. There is nothing, however, that will break down the barrier of over one hundred years that separates you from your soldier ancestor faster and more completely than to see and touch the gun that he shot, the clothes that he wore, and the letters that he wrote as he moved from one battlefield and campground to the next. A rifle stock worn smooth and polished bright by constant handling, a diary faded yellow with age whose contents will make a battle as fresh as today, a moth-eaten campaign hat with its cracked and warped leather visor, a sword with a stained blade and battered scabbard—these things will be the ultimate reality between you and your soldier, the final visible remains of your great-grandfather.

Of the millions of families descended from the soldiers in that war, only a bare fraction have such tangible reminders. Fortunately, there is a remarkable amount of equipment—guns, saddles, flags, books, knives—left from the war. There is plenty to go around, and the following pages will help relatives and collectors alike in locating and identifying just about any item they may want in the way of equipment similar to that which a particular soldier may have carried.

More than once I have had an enthusiastic relative bring out his grandfather's percussion sporting rifle or Spanish-American War surplus trap-door Springfield and, with misguided pride, parade it in front of me and the assembled guests as the gun that "Granpaw fought the Yankees with." And many more times I have seen and heard how a particular Knights of Columbus sword or a World War I officer's saber led troops that scaled a Union stronghold or sent the Rebels on a reverse trot in some bloody battle. These are not Civil War relics but were manufactured many years later and, as a consequence, they do not have the intrinsic value that a genuine Civil War antique has.

What follows, then, is a brief discussion on how to identify the most commonly used Civil War equipment, uniforms, belts, canteens, and weapons. The procedure will be almost all library or bookshop work to make you your own authority, for there are too many Civil War "experts" whose well-meaning ignorance will lead you into costly mistakes. Then too, unfortunately, the world of antiques has its share of predatory sharks and wolves who possess a razor-keen knowledge of your ancestor's equipment, firmly supported by a lack of moral scruples. These "experts" may strip you of your family treasures for a pittance or sell you a Civil War gun just like your father's father toted into battle, and you may find out too late that it was made up from parts in some basement or that you paid triple the price that you should have. The moral of the story, once again, is that it is far better, lacking honest and knowledgeable friends, to become knowledgeable yourself. It will in all probability save you many a heartache and a few friends, as well.

It would be impossible here to go into a detailed description of the innumerable varieties of Civil War weapons and accoutrements. There are, fortunately, a good many guides that will take you back to the products of the technical world of your ancestors of 1861–65. One of the best present-day general guides to identifying Civil War items is Dr. Francis A. Lord's *Civil War Collector's Encyclopedia*. Here is illustrated and described every kind of equipment from great to small: boarding axes, crutches, toothbrushes, pontoons, epaulettes, currycombs, hospital cars, coffeepots, tents, and more. This very helpful book is available from the Stackpole Company and is on the shelves of most state libraries.

This typical Confederate wooden barrel-stave canteen was owned by Private Florian Davis, 21st Louisiana Infantry. Davis was seriously wounded and later captured in the defense of Vicksburg. He was paroled by the federal army on promise never to bear arms against the Union. He kept his promise.

In 1865 Francis Bannerman established his "Military Goods Business," Francis Bannerman Sons, Inc. His was one of the most unusual business establishments ever organized in the United States. As a result of his shrewd buying not only of Civil War surplus material but of military equipment from all over the world, Bannerman became one of the great private arms suppliers of the world. He purchased an island in the Hudson River four miles north of West Point. He later transported a European castle, stone by stone, across the Atlantic and reassembled it on his island—an island upon and around which he dumped tons of cannon shells as support for his docks and warehouses. Bannerman was accused of being an "outfitter of revolutions," which he vigorously denied. The company has issued illustrated catalogs since 1884, and the most active imagination could not begin to conceive of the thousands upon thousands of varieties of equipment offered over the years. As a company, Bannerman's has declined from its palmy days, and most of the catalogs are costly collectors' items, but you can still get a modern 100th Anniversary representative catalog by writing to Francis Bannerman Sons, Inc., P. O. Box 26, Blue Point, Long Island, New York 11715. Bannerman catalogs, which cover weapons from over the entire world, are a prime source for identification of war material of any period of American history from the Spanish conquistadors through the Spanish-American War. You must get one of these catalogs to appreciate the fact that the foregoing comments are really an understatement.

Although "one picture is worth a thousand words" is a hopelessly overworked cliché, it is eminently true when you are trying to describe and identify equipment, particularly guns. James E. Serven's excellent book, *The Collecting of Guns,* is especially good for the beginner because of its many pictures, clear descriptive text, and good advice on what to look for, plus its very useful bibliography. It covers United States firearms from the flintlock to modern weapons. Another classic for beginners and professionals alike is Arcadi Gluckman's *Identifying Old U.S. Muskets,*

Rifles and Carbines. Gluckman will help you identify with pictures and text most rifles or muskets from 1803 to the modern army rifle. Gluckman's *United States Martial Pistols and Revolvers* is a splendid companion to *Identifying Old U.S. Muskets, Rifles and Carbines* and is every bit as competent.

James E. Hicks's *Notes on United States Ordnance: U.S. Military Firearms, 1776–1946* is a very useful book embellished by the beautiful and accurate drawings of André Jandot. For the uninitiated, "small arms" refers to long guns and short pistols. The very latest small arms book, and one of major significance, is Robert M. Reilly's *United States Military Small Arms, 1816–1865.* In all the literature in the field I believe there are no illustrations superior to Reilly's, and his text is clear, finely detailed, and authoritative. This is a book that has won deserved praise from the highest circles and is designed for both the rank amateur and the veteran collector. An extensive list of gun and equipment books, both old and new, is found in the back of this work. Although not yet widely distributed, it can readily be obtained through the Eagle Press, P. O. Box 198, Baton Rouge, Louisiana 70821.

The most authoritative books on Confederate weapons were written in whole or in part by that long-recognized dean of Rebel firearms, William Albaugh III, himself a direct descendant of two Confederate soldiers killed in the war. "Bill" Albaugh and Edward Simmons' *Confederate Arms,* Albaugh's *The Brass Framed Colt and Whitney,* Albaugh and Richard D. Steuart's *The Original Confederate Colt,* and Albaugh, Benet, and Simmons' *Confederate Handguns* may have equals, but I have yet to hear of them. Albaugh and his co-writers have done their task so well that subsequent hopeful writers on Southern arms must struggle under the burden of being "better than Albaugh."

A book that has gone through many printings, though it is not as useful nor as accurate as Reilly, Gluckman, Hicks, or Albaugh, is Charles Chapel's *Gun Collector's Handbook of Values.* The text is usually reliable, but the photographic illustrations are too small for detailed identification. This book, however, is one of the few that attempt to place a dollar value on a weapon—something that everyone wants to know. How much is grandfather's gun really worth? If the issue of Chapel that you are using is over a year old, many of the listed prices will not reflect a true value. E. Dixon Larson's *Colt Tips* is a good photographic book of Colt revolvers with their 1972 values. By far the best picture book of a collection of antique American handguns is *The William M. Locke Collection*, published by The Antique Armory, Inc., 2525 Main Street, East Point, Georgia 30344. It is unusual and especially good in identifying odd variations of Colts. Gun values are constantly changing—in almost all cases in an upward direction. A rare gun in poor condition will be beaten out in the price race every time by a less rare gun in fine condition.

There are a number of other ways to determine the value of firearms. One of the better dollar-value lists, and they are numerous, is that found in *The Gun Report,* an excellent monthly magazine devoted almost entirely to antique firearms. If you like antique weapons, you should take out a subscription to this modestly priced periodical.

Another value guide can be found by comparing prices of weapons for sale in *The Shotgun News*. This is a newspaper composed entirely of advertisements for antique weapons and accoutrements, Indian artifacts, modern war-surplus equipment, and the like. The National Rifle Association's publication, *The American Rifleman*, also carries lists of addresses of dealers and private collectors from whom weapons and other accoutrements can be purchased, as do a few other publications devoted to weap-

---

A page from Robert M. Reilly's book, United States Military Small Arms, 1816–1865, *showing in fine line drawings an accurate, detailed description of the Colt army model 1860 revolver, the most commonly used side arm in the Civil War, North or South. A highly desirable book for identifying rifles and handguns of the period 1816 to 1865.* ▶

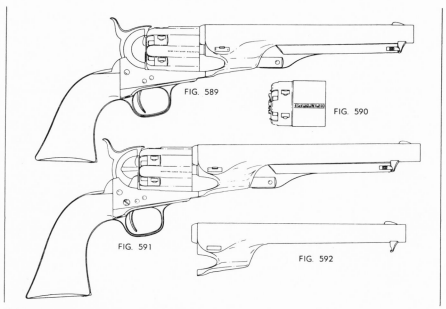

FIG. 589

FIG. 590

FIG. 591

FIG. 592

Model 1860 Armies were a very small number having a round, rebated cylinder of the type which later became standard. This cylinder appears in Figure 590.

Fluted cylinder Army revolvers, in all the variations noted above, dominate the first 2,000 arms of this model produced by Colt. After about serial number 2,000, the fluted cylinder declined substantially in numbers, and by the time 8,000 were turned out, this feature appears to have been completely superseded by the more common round, rebated cylinder. A small number are known in higher serial number ranges, but are believed to have been assembled with surplus parts.

The majority of the first 400 revolvers of this model were manufactured with 7-1/2-inch barrels, with both lengths utilized in nearly equal numbers through the remainder of production of the fluted cylinder types. The short barrel, however, is confined exclusively to these early model revolv-ers.

The fluted cylinder itself, designed primarily to reduce weight to a minimum, is believed to have been the suggestion of Wade Hampton of South Carolina, a man shortly thereafter to become a renowned Confederate cavalry commander.

In total, a maximum of 4,000 fluted cylinder Army revolvers appear to have been made. A few of these are known handsomely cased in pairs, or with a detachable shoulder stock, and an extreme few have been noted with tinned finishes.

These early Model 1860 Army revolvers, the Type I with "Navy" grips, and Type II comprising the remainder of fluted cylinder models, are believed to have been among the arms delivered under Colt's first contracts for "New Model Holster" revolvers.

• • •

COLT MODEL 1860 PERCUSSION ARMY REVOLVERS, TYPES III and IV

Caliber .44, rifled with 7 grooves having a left-hand twist. Length overall, 14 inches. Weight, 2 pounds, 11 ounces. Single-action.

The 8-inch barrel is round and finished blue. Two marking variations will be found, with the most common being "ADDRESS COL. SAML COLT NEW-YORK U.S. AMER-ICA". The other stamping is "ADDRESS SAML COLT HARTFORD CT." Both are one-line markings. A brass

blade front sight is 7/16 inch from the muzzle, and the rear sight is formed by a "V" notch in the hammer lip. As on the earlier types, a large loading groove extends completely through the rounded, somewhat streamlined barrel lug as may be seen in Figure 593. A very few of these revolvers, those fitted with detachable shoulder stocks, will be found with a small, two-leaf folding rear sight mortised into the top of the barrel at the breech. This feature is illustrated in

ons. Remember, however, that to place an accurate value on your gun or the weapon you wish to buy, you must do your homework well in Gluckman, Hicks, Reilly, or whatever reliable source you decide to use. The physical condition of the gun—is it rusted with parts missing, or is it complete with its original parts and free from corrosion?—these things are very important. You should understand that the absence of a screw or a difference in sight from one model to the next may mean a difference of hundreds of dollars. As an example, a standard .44-caliber Colt six-shooter issued to your great-uncle may have a smooth round cylinder (the place where you load the shells). The model made just before it looks identical with one exception: it does not have a smooth round cylinder but has a cylinder with a wavy surface made by grooves running down its length. The model with grooves is worth easily three times as much as the smooth-cylinder model. Almost every type of weapon has some distinguishing characteristics that alter its value from model to model, even though the models may look identical to an untrained eye.

The best book on U.S. Army and Militia swords is the old standby, *The American Sword, 1775–1945,* by Harold L. Peterson, the outstanding authority on U.S. "blades." This complete work will identify any U.S. Army sword, as the title suggests, from 1775 to 1945. If you own a sword and do not know how to identify it, most large libraries have a copy of Peterson to which you can refer. If yours is a Confederate sword, you will not find your "child" in *The American Sword.* Again, you must turn to William Albaugh; his work on Confederate swords is outstanding. His *Confederate Swords,* together with *Confederate Edged Weapons* and *A Photographic Supplement of Confederate Swords,* is the best you can get for the present.

In Appendix D you will find a partial list from Reilly's *U.S. Military Small Arms, 1816–1865,* which gives almost all the better books in the arms field. Serven's *Collecting of Guns* has a similar listing.

The two most reliable ways of obtaining a piece of Civil War equipment are through mail-order dealers who specialize in Civil War items, and at local and regional gun shows, where dealers and private collectors display, in addition to guns, letters, diaries, money, bugles, pictures, and a great variety of other reminders of those far-off days.

By mail order you can purchase almost anything you desire and more than you can imagine. The most important dealers advertise in the leading gun and antique magazines. *The Gun Report*, P. O. Box 111, Aledo, Illinois 61231, as mentioned before, is a high-quality monthly magazine dedicated to antique firearms and related items. A similar magazine of equal quality is the well-known *Arms Gazette*, Wallace Beinfeld Publications, Inc., 13222 Sapicoy Street, North Hollywood, California 91605. It is a truly fine source of information on antique and modern arms. Both magazines are reliable guides for anyone wishing to purchase Civil War items through the mail. Almost all the nationally known mail-order dealers advertise in them. Although the great majority of smaller dealers are honest and reliable, anyone purchasing by mail an item about which he knows very little might consider using the larger firms first. My only strong caution about mail-order buying by the inexperienced is, do not buy from the private individual selling one or two items from his "own collection" until you have the knowledge and ability to defend yourself. Private buying by mail is a chancy game in which you must carefully decide what risks you are willing to take.

Another satisfactory way of acquiring military equipment is at gun shows, a unique American institution. The better ones are an oriental bazaar and museum all in one. There are at least one or two of these shows somewhere in the United States each and every weekend in the year, and they are growing in popularity.

Local shows are sponsored by local gun clubs or civic organizations and national ones by large gun clubs. Gun shows are almost universally held on weekends, all day Saturday and part of Sunday, closing Sunday afternoon. Most are open to the public for a small fee. The size of a show is determined by the number of tables upon which the articles are displayed. A small local show will have maybe thirty tables. A giant national show will have up to one thousand. The shows are held in well-guarded auditoriums, dining halls, and ballrooms, for at a large show you will see literally several million dollars worth of guns and antiques associated with every aspect of American history. Of course, the emphasis is on the military.

A really good show will have many special educational display tables. Here you will see Civil War uniforms, Revolutionary War powder flasks, Confederate and Union cannon shells, even Indian artifacts. The variety is endless. The great majority of tables are sales tables operated mostly by small dealers and private collectors, with the larger dealers present in proportion to the size of the show.

Gun shows have the advantage of letting you see any number of swords—or whatever you desire—in a competitive atmosphere, as well as offering you the opportunity to meet some knowledgeable new friends who will be glad to help if they can. Once again, if you have done your homework and know what you are looking for, you might deal at first with small dealers and individuals. But remember, large, well-known dealers with good reputations and a knowledgeable friend to steer you away from fakes or overpriced relics are your best bets.

The Gun Report regularly lists all the gun shows occurring throughout the country so that you may see where and when the nearest ones will be held.

The American Rifleman, journal of the National Rifle Association, 1600 Rhode Island Avenue, Washington, D.C. 20036, has authoritative articles on antique guns and publishes, as well, supplemental handbooks, reprints, and the like. As an example, for a modest fee you can purchase reprint #7, *Civil War Small Arms,* which gives descriptions and photographs of rifles, carbines, and handguns. Then there is the pamphlet, *Gun Collec-*

tors Handbook, and several others that are useful in the weapons field. *The American Rifleman* also carries advertisements of gun sales and announcements of gun shows.

My first equipment buying experience was a traumatic one. I had longed to own a revolver similar to the one I knew my great-grandfather must have carried in the Civil War. When I saw my first Union army Colt lying in a showcase window, I was literally hypnotized by that vision of delight with its shiny, blued barrel, really beautiful grips, and sleek lines. The gun was at last mine for $200, which I could ill afford. I consulted no books and none of my friends until long after the sale. The gun, I learned later, had been recently reblued; the grips were modern bird's-eye maple, not the old, original Civil War walnut; and the serial numbers did not match, indicating that the gun had been made up from parts both new and old. It took me over a year to sell that bitter monument to my ignorance. I finally sold the gun for $70 and was lucky to do so.

One of the purposes of this chapter has been to steer you around such pitfalls. You will, if you do much collecting or selling of Civil War equipment, make mistakes, but if you are armed by patient reading and inquiry, all your mistakes will, I hope, be little ones.

8 / Examples of Research

A name is seldom enough.

My great-grandfather Groene marched away to war in the ranks of an Ohio or Indiana infantry regiment. Or was it an Illinois artillery battery? At any rate, he died during the war and left great-grandmother and two children to shift for themselves. Now, a little over a hundred years later, the family not only can't remember the state from which great-grandfather served, but no one can even recall his first name. Here is a difficult problem. It is a mystery and will probably remain so. I sent letters of inquiry to Indiana, Ohio, Michigan, etc. No great-grandfather. I looked in the *OR* and the *ORN* indexes. Still no luck. Was he an army, navy, or marine officer? I looked in F. B. Heitman's *Historical Register and Dictionary of the United States Army,* H. S. Hamersly's *Regular Army Register of the United States,* and L. R. Hamersly's *The Records of Military Officers of the United States Navy and Marine Corps.* I even looked in *Officers in the Confederate States Navy, 1861–1865,* from the United States Naval Records Office. But great-grandfather never trod the quarterdeck of a Confederate blockade runner or an ironclad ship. On my search went: libraries, museums, historical societies, special collections. Result—no records of a Groene north, south, or west.

Though my great-grandfather is lost to my family and to history, his is no isolated case. There are literally thousands of soldiers whose records have become misplaced, burned, lost, or otherwise destroyed. These men and their services and sacrifices are, and will probably remain, unknown.

I once owned a Civil War officer's sword with the inscription, "Presented to Lt. J. Wills by Stephen Mercer, Andrew N. Kennedy and others." The blade of this sword might just as well have been inscribed with the rest of the nine hundred or so men of the regiment for all the help it was to me. There were well over three thousand regiments, North and South. I searched through the standard officer biographies mentioned in a previous chapter and then abandoned the hunt. With nothing to go on but a name, you are in an almost impossible situation.

The moral to be drawn by antique collectors from the preceding example is never to consider paying extra for just a name on an antique unless the seller is willing to give you time to try to identify the man. An untraceable name adds nothing to the value of an antique, whether it be weapon, painting, letters, military equipment, or whatever.

Any clue to a name will help.

Occasionally there will be clues that will lead you directly to the identification of a soldier of whom you have only the name. A friend of mine owns a packet of Civil War letters, each signed by William Sullivan, regiment and state unknown. This soldier's frequent mention of friends in a nearby Michigan regiment moved me to write to the Michigan State Archives in Jackson on the chance that Sullivan's regiment was also from Michigan. It proved to be so—the Twenty-sixth Michigan Volunteer Infantry. There then unfolded a poignant story of how a nineteen-year-old farmer, Private William Sullivan, went south to save the Union and died of typhoid fever on the very day that his regiment marched off to battle in Virginia.

A Union officer's sword in front of me has inscribed on the brass throat at the top of the leather scabbard, "Presented to Lieut. C. S. Aldrich by his Ontario Friends." A search of the *OR* and Hamersly for Lieutenant Aldrich led nowhere, and I was miles from a set of the *Official Army Register of the Volunteer Forces of the United States Army.* The only clue was the word "Ontario." Since the soldier was probably not Canadian, I eliminated Ontario, Canada. That left Ontario, U.S.A., of which there are three or four. I began with Ontario, New York. I drove to the library, strolled over to that well-known six-volume set dedicated to New York Officers and Regiments, Phisterer's *New York in the War of the Rebellion.* (You would have found out about this set of books by referring to Dornbusch's section on

New York.) There I found a very brief military biography of Chauncey S. Aldrich. At twenty-seven he enlisted as a first lieutenant of Company B, Eighty-fifth New York Infantry. He later was adjutant of the regiment for a few months, and finally was promoted to Captain of Company B. He was mustered out as a major at the end of a three-year enlistment on December 16, 1864. In addition, Phisterer gave a brief history of the battles and casualties of the Eighty-fifth. I could have also found this regiment's history from Dyer's *Compendium.*

The Eighty-fifth up to April, 1864, was almost a noncombatant regiment. Then, suddenly, between April 17 and 20 the record lists 543 casualties, all missing! The whole regiment has disappeared at Plymouth, North Carolina. Fascinated by such a drastic change of events, I moved down half an aisle to where the *OR* and the *ORN* were shelved. I reached for the *OR*'s index volume, ran my finger down the pages to Plymouth, North Carolina, and jotted down the volumes in which Plymouth was mentioned. In less than one hour I had uncovered the whole dramatic story.

The Eighty-fifth New York was part of the troops garrisoning the Union fort at Plymouth, North Carolina, on the Roanoke River. On April 17, Confederate troops launched an attack to retake the town and fort, long held by the enemy. On April 19, the great Confederate ironclad battleship *Albemarle,* under Commander Cooke, closed in on the Union ships and fort, sank the U.S.S. *Southfield,* and drove away the smaller defending Union ships. The heavily outnumbered Union troops held to their fort until all hope was lost. Aldrich and his fellow officers handed over their swords to their Confederate captors, and the regiment laid down their weapons. For the Eighty-fifth New York the fighting was over, but not the dying. The 478 enlisted men were marched to traincars, where they were carried to Georgia and the infamous Andersonville Prison. Here, in less than a year, over half of them died. The twenty-two officers were more fortunate. They were sent south to Charleston and Columbia, South Carolina. All of this history was obtained in one afternoon in the

Louisiana State University Library. You could do as much in a smaller library.

My search was not yet ended. I next sent off two GSA 6751 forms, one requesting all records, and one requesting any medical records. Two months later in came the results, giving a pension record, any number of muster rolls, a company muster-in roll, a special muster roll, and last—real pay dirt—a memorandum of prisoner of war records. Captain Aldrich was taken to Columbia, South Carolina, and put in a prison compound. Here he escaped on October 11. One month and three days later he reported for duty in Knoxville, Tennessee.

The last and best part of the story, the escape, still remained to be told. A quick check in Dornbusch showed nothing written by Aldrich, and there were no regimental histories of the Eighty-fifth. I rechecked in Phisterer's *New York in the War of the Rebellion* and copied the officers' roster of the Eighty-fifth to see if any of Aldrich's companions wrote anything. I took the list back to Dornbusch and looked in the New York section. I was in luck. Captain D. A. Langworth of the Eighty-fifth wrote a book entitled *Reminiscences of a Prisoner of War and His Escape.* Maybe Langworth knew Aldrich. Dornbusch indicated that a copy of this book was located in the Library of Congress. DLC was the symbol. Through interlibrary loan I was able to have the book within three weeks. The result: Not only did Langworth know Aldrich; they escaped together! Here was a *whole book* on the perils and narrow escapes of Aldrich, Langworth, and three other officers, which included a photograph of the five taken just after their escape over the mountains of North Carolina into Union-held Tennessee.

Now the sword has a long pedigree and has become an incontestable part of a real-life drama played out over one hundred years ago, beginning with a besieged fort in North Carolina and ending in a Hollywood-scenario escape many months later.

Another weapon I considered buying, also a Union officer's sword, had inscribed on its brass guard "Captain Robert P.

MEMORANDUM FROM PRISONER OF WAR RECORDS.

No. _____

(This blank to be used only in the arrangement of said records.)

NAME.	RANK.	ORGANIZATION.				INFORMATION OBTAINED FROM—			
		No. of Reg't.	State.	Arm of Service.	Co.	Records of—	Vol.	Page.	Vol.	Page.

Aldrich C. S. — Captain — 80 — N.Y. — Vol. — 1 — C. S. Prisoner Case — 6 — 2 — Letters

Captured at _Columbia, S.C._ _Apr. 20_ , 186_4_, confined at Richmond, Va., _____ , 186 .

Admitted to Hospital at _____ , 186 , of _____

where he died _____ , 186 ; reported at Camp Parole, Md., _____ , 186 .

Paroled at _____

Escaped at Columbia, S.C. Oct. 11/64 reported at Provost Marshal, Knoxville Tenn. Nov. 13/64

Copied by _____ W.M.

Prisoner of War memorandum. This states that Capt. C. S. Aldrich of the 85th New York Infantry "escaped at Columbia, S. C., Oct. 11, 1864, and reported [10] Provost Marshal General, Knoxville Tenn. Nov. 13, 1864." Such information you can get only by a request for "all available information" from the government files. (See page 15.) Courtesy of the National Archives.

CAPTAIN C. S. ALDRICH AND HIS FRIENDS AS THEY APPEARED AFTER
REACHING THE UNION LINES
(From left to right) Lieut. J. E. Terwilliger, 85th N.Y.; Capt. C. S.
Aldrich, 85th N.Y.; Capt. D. A. Langworthy, 85th N.Y.; Lieut. G. S.
Hastings, 24th N.Y. Batt.; Capt. George H. Starr, 104th N.Y.

---

*"To Lt. C. S. Aldrich from his Ontario Friends" was the only identi-
fying clue inscribed on the scabbard of a Union officer's sword.
Research brought out an intriguing story of battle, capture, impris-
onment, and finally escape for Captain C. S. Aldrich of the 85th New
York Infantry and his companions shown above.*

Barry"—nothing else. Should I buy it or not? I took a quick look in Heitman to see if by chance it could belong to a regular officer. Luckily, Barry was listed. Now to the Index of the *OR*. There were nine pages of records: Breveted major for gallantry at Murfreesboro, taken prisoner, paroled, commanded the Sixteenth United States Regulars on Sherman's march to and siege of Atlanta. Needless to say, I bought the weapon.

About five years ago I purchased the sword of a George W. Bigham, Captain of Company F, Twenty-sixth Mississippi Infantry. Anxious for information, I dropped a letter to the Mississippi Department of Archives and History and received a quick reply, which stated only that he was Captain of Company F, Twenty-sixth Mississippi Infantry. I opened my copy of Dornbusch and turned to Mississippi. I found that there were no books or articles on the Twenty-sixth. However, at the beginning of each state, Dornbusch lists some general references. I copied down the three references for Mississippi and went to my state library. (If you aren't near one you can get the books by interlibrary loan.) Fortunately, one of the references, *Military Annals of Mississippi*, by John C. Rietti, was on the shelf. Here I struck a gold mine. I learned of Bigham's promotion from second to first lieutenant and of how, after the death of the company captain at the battle of Weldon's Railroad during the siege of Petersburg, he became Captain of Company F. Following this was a detailed history of every battle and skirmish of the Twenty-sixth. On May 5 and 6 Company F and the Twenty-sixth were among General Stone's four Mississippi regiments that finally stood in the Battle of the Wilderness, almost alone in the face of Grant's huge Federal army, until Longstreet came on the field. They fought at Tully's Mill, May 10; Spottsylvania Courthouse, May 22; Hanover Junction, May 23; Cold Harbor, June 2 and 3; Gaines' Mill, May 5; Weldon's Railroad, August 18–19; Fort McRae, October 1; and Hatcher's Run, October 27; in addition, they took part in many other skirmishes and fought in the entrenched lines at the final siege of Petersburg. All this I learned

(Confederate.)

13 | 26 | Miss.

George W. Bigham

2 *Corpl.* { Co. F (Anna Terry Guards),
26 Reg't Mississippi Volunteers.

Appears on a

"Record"*

of the organization named above,

from Sept. 1, 1861, to March 25, 1865.

Record dated: Near Petersburg, Va., March 16, 1865.

Enlisted:
When _Sept 1_ , 186 _1_.
Where _Iuka_
Period _3 yrs_

Born—(State)
Occupation _Farmer_
Residence—(Nearest P.O.) _Corinth_
Age when enlisted _21_
Married or single _S_
Remarks: _Promoted to 3 Sgt Sep 62_
Promoted to 2 Lt Nov 63 Promoted
to 1 Lt Dec 63 Promoted to Cap
Sep 1 1864

* From copy (made in the M. S. Office, War Department, in March, 1905,) of an original record borrowed from the Director of Archives and History, Jackson, Miss.—M. S. 938010.

Book mark:

Wm Potter

(654)   [OVER]   Copyist.

APR. 23   47739027   1907.

ENGAGEMENTS.*

Fort Donelson, Feb. 13, 1862
Fort Donelson, Feb. 14, 1862
Fort Donelson, Feb. 15, 1862
Surrendered, Feb. 16, 1862
Coffeeville, Dec. 5, 1862
Skirmish, Willow Springs, May 3, 1863
Baker's Creek, May 16, 1863
Jackson, Miss., from July 9 to 16, 1863
Wilderness, May 5, 1864
Wilderness, May 6, 1864
Tally's Mill, May 10, 1864
Spottsylvania Court House, May 12, 1864
Hanover Junction, May 23, 1864
Cold Harbor, June 2, 1864
Cold Harbor, June 3, 1864
Gaines' Mill, from June 5 to 13, 1864
In front of Petersburg, July 4 to Aug. 17, 1864
Weldon R. R., Aug. 18, 1864
Weldon R. R., Aug. 19, 1864
In front of Petersburg, Aug. 20 to Sept. 29, 1864
Skirmish, Oct. 2, 1864
Hatcher's Run, Oct. 27, 1864
Jarratt's Station, Dec. 10, 1864
Hatcher's Run, Feb. 6, 1865
Fort McRae, Oct. 1, 1864
Fight with deserters near Ellisville, Dec. 23, 1863

*The following characters mean: P. present and unhurt; w. wounded; s. w. severely wounded; k. killed; a. absent without leave; a. f. absent on furlough or satisfactorily; a. d. absent on detail or duty by order; a. s. absent sick; s. w. absent wounded; a. c. absent captured; a. a. absent under arrest; c. captured; x. deserted; m. missing; p. d. present detailed; m. w. mortally wounded. Those marked thus (*) in column of names, re-enlisted under Act of December 11, 1861, or were held in service by Act of April 16, 1862.

The National Archives records are very inconsistent in content. The above items on George W. Bigham, Captain, Co. F, 26th Mississippi, illustrate this point. The "Record" is often found in a soldier's folder. The list of "Engagements" in which he participated is not often found so completely done. Courtesy of the National Archives.

the first day at the library. My next step should have been to write for Bigham's pension record, but I had enough to satisfy my curiosity.

In some cases there is almost too much information to bother with. The reader will recall the young artillery officer, Ebenezer Mason, in Chapter I, whose battery helped stop the Confederate flotilla as it steamed down the James River on that freezing January night in 1865. At the conclusion of the search for Mason's story I had done the following:

1. Written a letter to the Connecticut State Adjutant General's Office and received one page of records giving his enlistment dates, promotions, discharge, and burial data. Cost: one eight-cent stamp.

2. Filled out one GSA 6751 form checking pension records and written across the top of the form, "Send all Pension Records." Result: eight pages of pension records giving a complete summary of his service in the First Connecticut Heavy Artillery and a summary of his life as a veteran after the war, including the time, place, and nature of his death. Cost: $1.50.

3. Filled out one GSA 6751 form and written across the top, "Send all military records." Result: thirty-nine sheets of various muster rolls, three sheets of other records. Total cost: $6.00.

4. Checked in Dornbusch, which revealed eight references to histories, rosters, etc., of the First Connecticut Heavy Artillery. Made a trip to my library, where an interlibrary loan request was mailed to the Connecticut State Library for John C. Taylor's *History of the First Connecticut Artillery and of the Siege Trains of the Armies Operating against Richmond, 1862–1865*. On receiving the book I copied eight pages of notes relating directly to Mason. Left untouched were the seven other books, etc., on the First Artillery. Cost: $1.75.

5. Checked the *OR* and *ORN*, which revealed eighteen pages of reports and records relating to Mason and his participation in various engagements. Cost: nothing.
6. Checked Dyer's *Compendium,* which gave one paragraph of the history of the regiment. Cost: nothing.

In total I collected seventy-eight pages of records at a cost of around $9.00. There are undoubtedly many more pages on Mason in the seven Dornbusch references that I did not bother to send for, but seventy-eight pages of references to my soldier and his sword are quite enough for me for now. I'll tackle the rest on some distant rainy day.

There are times in historical research when nothing seems to help, even when the complete name and regiment are known. I know of a battered and bloody battle drum with "Chester Chitfield, 29 Ohio Volunteer Infantry," plainly written on the inside of the rounded body. Written on the snarehead side of the drum are the proud but faded words: "Fredericksburgh Va. Dec. 13–14, 1862," and "Chancellorsville, May 3rd 1863." One-third of the drum or batterhead side is stained with blood. There is no record of a Chester Chitfield on the existing rolls of the Twenty-ninth Ohio Volunteer Infantry, yet the drum is authentic beyond the shadow of a doubt.

The grandfather of an acquaintance of mine was in the Rebel army that defended Vicksburg against Grant's besieging army in 1863. His name does not appear on the rolls of the Confederate regiment in which the family knows that he served. This lack of records means nothing since the grandfather's name and regiment are chiseled in stone on one of Vicksburg's many monuments for all the world to see. The simple fact, as I have said before, is that records do get lost by the tens of thousands. If you cannot find information on your soldier, it does not mean that he never existed. It means only that he was, historically speaking, shot dead in the records office. So you must brace yourself for occasional failures and dead ends.

This picture shows the strokes of the sticks in the center of the drum and the bloodstains of the drummer around the edge. On the other side of the drum is written, "Fredericksburgh Va. Dec. 13–14, 1862," and "Chancellorsville, May 3rd 1863." Inside the drum in pencil is inscribed the name of the drummer and his Ohio regiment. No trace can be found of this drummer's record, though it is obvious that he and his drum were in the war.

Often a family's handed-down history will appear to have hardly a word of truth in it. A beautiful Colt Civil War army revolver I own came with a wonderful story. The owner, Captain Charles P. Crandall, had been on the personal staff of Robert E. Lee. Crandall, I was told, was a trusted friend whom the great general sent upon many an important mission, both as his courier and as his personal representative. This story was related by Crandall's aging widow in the depression days of the 1930's. She was selling the last mementos of her long-dead husband to hold her poor old body and soul together. A search into the records found that Charles P. Crandall was a private in the First Virginia Artillery—that and nothing more.

A year or so ago an old friend of mine, Paul Hobday, died at the age of ninety-three. Paul's father, Charles Hobday, had been a trooper in the Fifth Virginia Cavalry. On many a wintry day I would sit by Paul's chair in front of an old oil stove and listen to him retell the tales of that far-off war recounted to him by his father. I would occasionally glance over my shoulder to catch a glimpse of an old cavalry sword that was hanging over the door behind us. Perhaps it was to reassure myself that what I was hearing was really true. Maybe it was simply to lay my eyes upon that old weapon to make more real the story being told me by an old man who I knew would soon be dead. At any rate, I occasionally broke the spell to jot a few quick notes. Later I collected a bit more family data. Paul died, and I bought that sword above the door. All the records that I could ever obtain of Paul's father were two pages of a company muster roll stating that Private Charles E. Hobday transferred from the Sixty-first Virginia Militia to the Fifth Virginia Cavalry on May 14, 1862. How many of the stories that Paul told me as we sat together in front of that stove while the cold January winds swept up the East River from Mobjack Bay, Virginia, were true, I shall never know. I shall never know since the records are silent and I must trust to an old man's memory that most likely quickened and brightened each story with its retelling. I shall never forget those days, as you will never forget stories told to you by your grand old folk, and you, like me, may be reluctant to dig into the cold facts, for so often dreams are a better reality. But you must, you know, for grandfather may not have told half the story, and that untold story may be the best part of all.

Institutions That Hold Microfilmed Service Records from the National Archives

ALABAMA
CONFEDERATE VOLUNTEERS
   Birmingham Public Library, Birmingham
   United Daughters of the Confederacy, Richmond, Virginia
UNION VOLUNTEERS*
   Auburn University, Auburn
   Birmingham Public Library, Birmingham

ARIZONA TERRITORY
CONFEDERATE VOLUNTEERS
   Arizona State College, Flagstaff
   Arizona Historical Foundation, Tempe
   University of Arizona, Tucson
   Fort Lewis College, Durango
   Arlington State College, Tennessee
   Salt Lake City Genealogical Society, Salt Lake City, Utah
   United Daughters of the Confederacy, Richmond, Virginia

ARKANSAS
CONFEDERATE VOLUNTEERS
   Arkansas History Commission, Little Rock
   United Daughters of the Confederacy, Richmond, Virginia
UNION VOLUNTEERS
   Arkansas History Commission, Little Rock

FLORIDA
CONFEDERATE VOLUNTEERS
   University of Florida, Gainesville
   Hillsborough County Historical Commission, Tampa
   United Daughters of the Confederacy, Richmond, Virginia

*Union Volunteers refers to men from Southern states who fought in the ranks of the Union army.

UNION VOLUNTEERS
  University of Florida, Gainesville

GEORGIA
CONFEDERATE VOLUNTEERS
  Department of Archives and History, Atlanta
  United Daughters of the Confederacy, Richmond, Virginia
UNION VETERANS
  Department of Archives and History, Atlanta

KENTUCKY
CONFEDERATE VOLUNTEERS
  Murray State University, Murray
  United Daughters of the Confederacy, Richmond, Virginia

LOUISIANA
CONFEDERATE VOLUNTEERS
  Louisiana State University, Baton Rouge
  Louisiana State Archives and Records Commission,
    Baton Rouge
  Louisiana Civil War Centennial Commission, Baton Rouge
  New Orleans Public Library, New Orleans
  United Daughters of the Confederacy, Richmond, Virginia
UNION VOLUNTEERS
  Louisiana State University, Baton Rouge
  Louisiana State Archives and Records Commission,
    Baton Rouge
  New Orleans Public Library, New Orleans

MARYLAND
CONFEDERATE VOLUNTEERS
  Maryland Historical Society, Baltimore
  United Daughters of the Confederacy, Richmond, Virginia

MISSISSIPPI
CONFEDERATE VOLUNTEERS
  Louisiana State University, Baton Rouge, Louisiana
  University of Southern Mississippi, Hattiesburg
  Department of Archives and History, Jackson
  United Daughters of the Confederacy, Richmond, Virginia

UNION VOLUNTEERS
  California State College, Hayward, California
  Louisiana State University, Baton Rouge, Louisiana
  University of Southern Mississippi, Hattiesburg

MISSOURI
CONFEDERATE VOLUNTEERS
  St. Louis Public Library
  United Daughters of the Confederacy, Richmond, Virginia
UNION VOLUNTEERS
  St. Louis Public Library

NEW MEXICO TERRITORY
UNION VOLUNTEERS
  University of New Mexico, Albuquerque
  Genealogical Society of the Church of Jesus Christ of Latter
    Day Saints, Salt Lake City, Utah

NORTH CAROLINA
CONFEDERATE VOLUNTEERS
  Office of Archives and History, Department of Art, Culture
    and History, Raleigh
  United Daughters of the Confederacy, Richmond, Virginia
UNION VOLUNTEERS
  Office of Archives and History, Department of Art, Culture
    and History, Raleigh

SOUTH CAROLINA
CONFEDERATE VOLUNTEERS
  United Daughters of the Confederacy, Richmond, Virginia

TENNESSEE
CONFEDERATE VOLUNTEERS
  Tennessee State Library and Archives, Nashville
  Cossitt-Goodwyn Libraries, Memphis
  United Daughters of the Confederacy, Richmond, Virginia
UNION VOLUNTEERS
  Tennessee State Library and Archives, Nashville

TEXAS

CONFEDERATE VOLUNTEERS
United Daughters of the Confederacy, Richmond, **Virginia**

UNION VOLUNTEERS
Rice University, Houston

UTAH

UNION VOLUNTEERS
Ricks College, Rexburg, Idaho
University of Nevada, Reno, Nevada
Salt Lake City Genealogical Society, Salt Lake City

VIRGINIA

CONFEDERATE VOLUNTEERS
Virginia Polytechnic Institute, Blacksburg
United Daughters of the Confederacy, Richmond
West Virginia Department of Archives and History,
    Charleston, West Virginia

UNION VOLUNTEERS
West Virginia Department of Archives and History,
    Charleston, West Virginia

CONFEDERATE GENERAL AND STAFF OFFICERS AND
NONREGIMENTAL ENLISTED MEN
University of British Columbia, Vancouver, B.C.
Georgia Department of Archives and History,
    Atlanta, Georgia
South Carolina Department of Archives and History,
    Columbia, South Carolina
United Daughters of the Confederacy, Richmond

ORGANIZATIONS RAISED DIRECTLY BY THE
CONFEDERATE GOVERNMENT
Georgia Department of Archives and History,
    Atlanta, Georgia
United Daughters of the Confederacy, Richmond

Appendix B/

Institutions That Hold Complete Sets of Indexes to Civil War Military Service Records

UNION SOLDIERS

ALABAMA
Auburn University, Auburn
Huntsville Public Library, Huntsville
Jacksonville State University, Jacksonville
Dallas Public Library, Dallas, Texas

ARIZONA TERRITORY
Arizona State College, Flagstaff
Arizona State University, Tempe
University of Arizona, Tucson
The Cox Library, Tucson
Ft. Lewis College, Durango, Colorado

ARKANSAS
Arkansas History Commission, Little Rock
Dallas Public Library, Dallas, Texas

CALIFORNIA
Arizona State University, Tempe, Arizona
California State Historical Society, Sacramento

COLORADO
Arizona State University, Tempe, Arizona
Colorado State Archives, Denver
Ft. Lewis College, Durango

CONNECTICUT
none

DAKOTA TERRITORY
State Historical Society, Fargo, North Dakota
Fargo Public Library, Fargo, North Dakota
University of North Dakota, Grand Fork, North Dakota
Karl E. Mundt Historical and Educational Foundation,
   Dakota State College, Madison, South Dakota

DELAWARE
  University of Delaware, Newark
DISTRICT OF COLUMBIA
  University of Alabama, University, Alabama
FLORIDA
  University of Florida, Gainesville
  Monroe County Public Library, Key West
GEORGIA
  University of Alabama, University, Alabama
  Georgia Department of Archives and History, Atlanta
  Dallas Public Library, Dallas, Texas
ILLINOIS
  Southern Illinois University, Carbondale
INDIANA
  none
IOWA
  University of Iowa, Ames
KANSAS
  Wichita Public Library, Wichita
KENTUCKY
  none
LOUISIANA
  Louisiana State University, Alexandria
  Louisiana State Library, Baton Rouge
  Louisiana State Archives and Records Commission,
    Baton Rouge
  St. Mary Parish Library, Franklin
  New Orleans Public Library, New Orleans
  Dallas Public Library, Dallas, Texas
MAINE
  none
MARYLAND
  none
MASSACHUSETTS
  none

MICHIGAN
   Western Michigan University, Kalamazoo
   Michigan State Library, Lansing
MINNESOTA
   none
MISSISSIPPI
   University of Alabama, University, Alabama
   Louisiana State University, Alexandria, Louisiana
   University of Southern Mississippi, Hattiesburg
   Dallas Public Library, Dallas, Texas
MISSOURI
   St. Louis Public Library, St. Louis
NEBRASKA TERRITORY
   none
NEVADA
   Arizona State University, Tempe, Arizona
NEW HAMPSHIRE
   none
NEW JERSEY
   none
NEW MEXICO TERRITORY
   Arizona Pioneer's Historical Society
   Ft: Lewis College, Durango, Colorado
   University of New Mexico, Albuquerque
   Texas Western College, El Paso, Texas
NEW YORK
   none
NORTH CAROLINA
   University of Alabama, University, Alabama
   Methodist College, Fayetteville
   Wake Forest University, Winston-Salem
   Dallas Public Library, Dallas, Texas
OHIO
   none

OREGON
  Idaho State University, Pocatello, Idaho
  Oregon Historical Society, Portland
  Oregon State Library, Salem
PENNSYLVANIA
  none
RHODE ISLAND
  Rhode Island Historical Society, Providence
TENNESSEE
  Tennessee State Library and Archives, Nashville
  Knoxville Public Library, Knoxville
TEXAS
  Texas State Library, Austin
  La Retama Public Library, Corpus Christi
  Dallas Public Library, Dallas
  Rice University, Houston
  Angelo State College, San Angelo
UTAH
  Ft. Lewis College, Durango, Colorado
  Idaho State University, Pocatello, Idaho
  Utah State University, Logan
  Brigham Young University, Provo
  Utah State Archives, Salt Lake City
  Laramie County Library, Cheyenne, Wyoming
VERMONT
  none
VIRGINIA
  Archives and History Department, Charleston, West **Virginia**
WASHINGTON TERRITORY
  Idaho State University, Pocatello, Idaho
  Oregon Historical Society, Portland, Oregon
WEST VIRGINIA
  West Virginia University, Morgantown
WISCONSIN
  none

COLORED TROOPS
  Florida State University, Tallahassee, Florida
  Tennessee State Library and Archives, Nashville, Tennessee

CONFEDERATE SOLDIERS

CONSOLIDATED
  Arkansas History Commission, Little Rock, Arkansas
  St. Louis Public Library, St. Louis, Missouri
  South Carolina Department of Archives and History,
    Columbia, South Carolina
ALABAMA
  Public Library of Anniston and Calhoun County, Anniston
  Huntsville Public Library, Huntsville
  University of Alabama, University
  Jacksonville State University, Jacksonville
  Houston Public Library, Houston, Texas
ARIZONA
  Arizona State College, Flagstaff
  Arizona Historical Foundation, Tucson
  University of Arizona, Tucson
  Fort Lewis College, Durango, Colorado
  Texas Western College, El Paso, Texas
ARKANSAS
  Arkansas Historical Commission, Little Rock
  Houston Public Library, Houston, Texas
FLORIDA
  University of Alabama, University, Alabama
  Florida State Genealogical Commission, Jacksonville
  University of Florida, Gainesville
  University of South Florida, Tampa
  Hillsborough County Historical Society, Tampa
GEORGIA
  University of Alabama, University, Alabama
  Georgia Department of Archives and History, Atlanta

KENTUCKY
  Murray State University, Murray
  Houston Public Library, Houston, Texas
LOUISIANA
  Louisiana State University, Alexandria
  Louisiana State Library, Baton Rouge
  Louisiana State Archives and Records Commission,
    Baton Rouge
  New Orleans Public Library, New Orleans
MARYLAND
  Houston Public Library, Houston, Texas
MISSISSIPPI
  University of Alabama, University, Alabama
  Florida State Genealogical Commission, Jacksonville, Florida
  Western Kentucky University, Bowling Green, Kentucky
  Louisiana State University, Alexandria, Louisiana
  University of Southern Mississippi, Hattiesburg
  Houston Public Library, Houston, Texas
MISSOURI
  Houston Public Library, Houston, Texas
NORTH CAROLINA
  University of Alabama, University, Alabama
SOUTH CAROLINA
  University of Alabama, University, Alabama
  Houston Public Library, Houston, Texas
TENNESSEE
  Tennessee Polytechnic Institute, Cookeville
  Knoxville Public Library, Knoxville
TEXAS
  La Retama Public Library, Corpus Christi
  Dallas Public Library, Dallas
  Fort Worth Public Library, Fort Worth
  Rice University, Houston
  Stephen F. Austin State College, Nacogdoches
  Angelo State College, San Angelo

VIRGINIA
   Virginia State Library, Richmond
   West Virginia Department of Archives and History,
      Charleston, West Virginia

Appendix C/
Source Books for Regimental Histories and Rosters*

ALABAMA

Brewer, Willis. *Alabama, Her History, Resources, War Record, and Public Men, from 1540 to 1872.* Montgomery, Alabama: Barrett and Brown, 1872.

ARIZONA

See adjacent states.

ARKANSAS

Ferguson, John L., ed. *Arkansas and the Civil War.* Little Rock, Arkansas: Pioneer Press, 1965.

Arkansas Adjutant General's Office. *Report of the Adjutant General of the State of Arkansas, for the Period of the Late Rebellion, and to November 1, 1866.* Washington, D. C.: Government Printing Office, 1867.

CALIFORNIA

Hunt, Aurora. *The Army of the Pacific.* Glendale, California: A. H. Clark Co., 1951.

Orton, Richard H., compiler. *Records of California Men in the War of the Rebellion, 1861–1867.* Sacramento, California: State Printer, 1890.

Rogers, Fred B. *Soldiers of the Overland.* San Francisco, California: The Grabhorn Press, 1938.

Adjutant General's Office. *Official Army Register of the Volunteer Force of the United States Army for the Years 1861,'62, '63,'64,'65.* Part VII. Washington, D. C.: Government Printing Office, 1869.

*This list is a quick reference for those who wish the most complete and authoritative state regimental and state roster source books in one or several volumes. They have been recommended chiefly by the various state archives and historical societies. For detailed works see C. E. Dornbusch, *Military Bibliography of the Civil War,* and Nevins, Robertson, and Wiley, *Civil War Books.*

COLORADO

Hollister, Ovando. *Colorado Volunteers in New Mexico, 1862.* Chicago, Illinois: R. R. Donnelley, 1962.

Naukwell, John H. *History of the Military Organizations of Colorado, 1860–1935.* Denver, Colorado: W. H. Kistler Stationery Co., 1935.

Adjutant General's Office. *Official Army Register of the Volunteer Force of the United States Army for the Years 1861,'62, '63,'64,'65.* Part VIII. Washington, D. C.: Government Printing Office, 1869.

Colorado State Archives and Public Records. Department of Military Affairs. *Biennial Reports of the Adjutant General, 1861–1865.* Denver, Colorado: Adjutant General's Office, 1866.

CONNECTICUT

Adjutant General's Office. *The Record of Connecticut Men in the War of Rebellion, 1861–1865.* Hartford, Conn.: Press of Case, Lockwood and Brainard Co., 1889.

DELAWARE

Scharf, J. Thomas. *History of Delaware, 1609–1888.* Two volumes. Philadelphia, Pa.: L. J. Richards and Co., 1888.

Adjutant General's Office. *Official Army Register of the Volunteer Forces of the United States Army for the Years 1861,'62, '63,'64,'65.* Part III. Washington, D. C.: United States Government Printing Office, 1869.

FLORIDA

Robertson, Frederick L. *Soldiers of Florida in the Seminole Indian, Civil and Spanish-American Wars.* Live Oak, Florida: Democrat Book and Job Print., 1909.

GEORGIA

Dornbusch, C. E. *Military Bibliography of the Civil War.* Volume 2, Georgia. New York: New York Public Library, 1967.

Garman, Edward. "Materials for the Writing of Histories of Georgia Confederate Regiments: A Bibliographic Study." Master's thesis, University of Georgia, n.d.

Henderson, Lillian. *Roster of the Confederate Soldiers of Georgia.* Six volumes. Hapeville, Georgia: Longino and Porter, 1959–64.

ILLINOIS

Reece, J. N. *Adjutant General's Reports for the Years 1861–66.* Eight volumes. Springfield, Illinois: Phillips Bros., State Printers, 1900–02.

INDIANA

McCormick, David. *Indiana Battle Flags.* Indianapolis, Indiana: Indiana Battle Flag Commission, 1929.

Terrell, W. H. H. *Adjutant General's Report.* Eight volumes. Indianapolis, Indiana: Alexander H. Conner, State Printer, 1865–69.

Turner, Ann. *Guide to Indiana Civil War Manuscripts.* Indianapolis, Indiana: Indiana Civil War Centennial Commission, 1965.

IOWA

Petersen, William J. *Iowa History Reference Guide.* Iowa City, Iowa: The State Historical Society of Iowa, 1952.

Thrift, William H. *Roster and Record of Iowa Soldiers in the War of the Rebellion.* Six volumes. Des Moines, Iowa: E. H. English, State Printer, 1908.

KANSAS

Adjutant General. *Report of the Adjutant General of the State of Kansas, 1861–65.* Topeka, Kansas: Kansas State Print. Co., 1896.

KENTUCKY

Speed, Thomas, *et al. The Union Regiments of Kentucky.*

Louisville, Kentucky: Union Soldiers and Sailors Monument Association, Courier-Journal Job Print. Co., 1897.

Adjutant General's Office. *Report of the Adjutant General of the State of Kentucky. Confederate Kentucky Volunteers, War 1861–1865.* Two volumes. Frankfort, Kentucky: State Journal Co., Printers, 1915–18.

LOUISIANA

Booth, Andrew. *Records of Louisiana Confederate Soldiers and Louisiana Confederate Commands.* New Orleans, Louisiana: Military Record Commission, 1920.

MAINE

Jordan, W. B. *Maine in the Civil War: A Bibliographic Guide.* Portland, Maine: Maine Historical Society, n.d. ($2.00 per copy from Maine Historical Society, 485 Congress Street, Portland, Maine.)

Whitman, E. S., and True, Charles H. *Maine in the War for the Union. History of the Part Borne by Maine Troops in the Suppression of the American Rebellion.* Lewiston, Maine: Nelson Dingley, Jr., and Co., Publishers, 1865.

Adjutant General's Office. *Annual Report, 1861–66.* Seven volumes. Augusta, Maine: Stevens and Sayward, 1862–67.

MARYLAND

Goldsborough, William W. *The Maryland Line in the Confederate Army, 1861–1865.* (Confederate) Baltimore, Maryland: Press of Guggenheimer, Weil and Co., 1900.

State Commissioners. *The History and Roster of Maryland Volunteers, War of 1861–5.* Volumes 1 and 2. Baltimore, Maryland: Press of Guggenheimer, Weil and Co., 1898–99.

MASSACHUSETTS

Higginson, Thomas W. *Massachusetts in the Army and Navy*

During the War of 1861–1865. Two volumes. Boston, Massachusetts: Wright & Potter, 1895–96.

Adjutant General's Office. *The Massachusetts Soldiers, Sailors and Marines in the Civil War.* Eight volumes. Norwood, Massachusetts: At the Norwood Press, 1931.

MICHIGAN

Brown, George H., ed. *Record of Service of Michigan Volunteers in the Civil War, 1861–1865.* 46 volumes. Kalamazoo, Michigan: Ihling Bros. and Everard Printers, 1905.

Robertson, John. *Michigan in the War.* Lansing, Michigan: W. S. George and Co., State Printers, 1882.

MINNESOTA

Board of Commissioners. *Minnesota in the Civil War and Indian War, 1861–1865.* Two volumes. St. Paul, Minnesota: Pioneer Press Co., 1890–93.

MISSISSIPPI

Rietti, John C. *Military Annals of Mississippi.* Jackson, Mississippi: Published by the author, 1895.

Rowland, Dunbar. "Military History of Mississippi," *Official and Statistical Register of the State of Mississippi.* Pp. 387–943. Nashville, Tennessee: Dept. Archives and History, 1908.

MISSOURI

Dyer, Frederick H. *A Compendium of the War of the Rebellion.* Volume III. New York: Thomas Yoseloff, 1959.

Adjutant General of Missouri Reports 1863–1865.

United States Records and Pension Office. *Organization and Status of Missouri Troops (Union and Confederate) in Service During the Civil War.* Washington, D. C.: Government Printing Office, 1902.

NEVADA

Dornbusch, C. E. *Military Bibliography of the Civil War.* Volume II, Nevada. New York: The New York Public Library, 1967.

Adjutant General's Office. *Official Army Register of the Volunteer Force of the United States Army for the Years 1861, '62, '63, '64, '65.* Part VII. Washington, D. C.: Government Printing Office, 1867.

NEW HAMPSHIRE

Ayling, Augustus. *Revised Register of New Hampshire Soldiers and Sailors in the War of the Rebellion.* Concord, New Hampshire: Ira C. Evans, Public Printer, 1895.

NEW JERSEY

Sinclair, Donald A. *The Civil War and New Jersey.* New Brunswick, New Jersey: Published by the Friends of the Rutgers University Library for the New Jersey Civil War Centennial Commission, 1968.

Stryker, William. *Records of Officers and Men of New Jersey in the Civil War 1861–1865.* Trenton, New Jersey: J. L. Murphy, 1876.

NEW MEXICO

Dornbusch, C. E. *Military Bibliography of the Civil War.* Volume II, New Mexico. New York: The New York Public Library, 1967.

Adjutant General's Office. *Official Army Register of the Volunteer Force of the United States Army for the Years 1861, '62, '63, '64, '65.* Part VIII. Washington, D. C.: Government Printing Office, 1869.

NEW YORK

Dornbusch, C. E. *Military Bibliography of the Civil War.* Volume I, New York. New York: The New York Public Library, 1967.

Phisterer, Frederick. *New York in the War of the Rebellion, 1861–1865.* Six volumes. Albany: J. B. Lyon Co., State Printers, 1912.

NORTH CAROLINA

Jordan, Weymouth T. and Manarin, Louis H. *North Carolina Troops 1861–1865.* Thirteen volumes. Raleigh, North Carolina: North Carolina Division of Archives and History, in publication.

Moore, John W. *Roster of North Carolina Troops in the War Between the States.* Raleigh, North Carolina: Ashe and Gatling, 1882.

NORTH DAKOTA

See South Dakota.

OHIO

Official Roster of Soldiers of the State of Ohio in the War of the Rebellion. Twelve volumes. Akron, Ohio: Werner Company, 1886–95.

Reid, Whitelaw. *Ohio in the War.* Two volumes. Cincinnati, Ohio: Moore, Wilstach and Baldwin, 1868.

OKLAHOMA

See adjacent states and territories in Dornbusch and Nevins, Robertson, and Wiley.

Foreman, Grant. *History of the Service and List of Individuals of the Five Civilized Tribes in the Confederate Army.* Two volumes. Oklahoma City, Oklahoma: Oklahoma Historical Society, 1928.

PENNSYLVANIA

Bates, Samuel P. *History of Pennsylvania Volunteers, 1861–1865.* Five volumes. Harrisburg, Pennsylvania: Harris B. Singerly, 1869–71.

RHODE ISLAND

Dyer, Elisha. *Adjutant General's Report of 1865.* Providence, Rhode Island: C. L. Freeman and Sons, 1893–95.

SOUTH CAROLINA

Dornbusch, C. E. *Military Bibliography of the Civil War.* Volume II, South Carolina. New York: The New York Public Library, 1967.

Easterby, J. H. *Guide to the Study and Reading of South Carolina History.* Spartanburg, South Carolina: Reprint Company. (For regimentals.)

NARS Microcopy 267, National Archives. (For rosters of South Carolina soldiers.)

SOUTH DAKOTA

English, M. A. "Dakota's First Soldiers," *South Dakota Historical Collection.* Volume IX. Pierre, South Dakota, 1918.

Jones, Robert Huhn. *The Civil War in the Northwest: Nebraska, Wisconsin, Iowa, Minnesota and the Dakotas.* Norman, Oklahoma: University of Oklahoma Press, 1960.

Monaghan, Jay. *The Civil War on the Western Border.* Boston, Massachusetts: Little, Brown and Co., 1955.

TENNESSEE

Lindsley, John B. *The Military Annals of Tennessee.* Nashville, Tennessee: J. M. Lindsley and Company, 1886.

Tennesseans in the Civil War. Nashville, Tennessee: Civil War Centennial Commission, 1964.

TEXAS

Wright, Marcus J. (Simpson, Harold B., ed.). *Texas in the War, 1861–1865.* Hillsboro, Texas: Hill Jr. College Press, 1965.

UTAH

Dornbusch, C. E. *Military Bibliography of the Civil War.*

(See adjacent western states and territories). Volumes I and II. New York: The New York Public Library, 1967.

VERMONT

Adjutant General. *Revised Roster of Vermont Volunteers of the Civil War.* Montpelier, Vermont: Press of the Watchman Publishing Co., 1892.

VIRGINIA

Dornbusch, C. E. *Military Bibliography of the Civil War.* Volume II, Virginia. New York: The New York Public Library, 1967.

Wallace, Lee A. *A Guide to Virginia Military Organizations, 1861–65.* Richmond, Virginia: Virginia Civil War Commission, 1964.

WEST VIRGINIA

Long, Theodore K. *Loyal West Virginians from 1861 to 1865.* Baltimore, Maryland: Deutsch Publishing Co., 1895.

Munn, Robert F. *West Virginia Civil War Literature.* Morgantown, West Virginia: West Virginia University Library, 1963.

WISCONSIN

Love, William D. *Wisconsin in the War of the Rebellion.* Chicago, Illinois: Church and Goodman, 1866.

Quiner, Edwin B. *Military History of Wisconsin.* Chicago, Illinois: Clarke and Co., 1866.

Wisconsin Adjutant General. *Roster of Wisconsin Volunteers, War of the Rebellion, 1861–1865.* Two volumes. Madison, Wisconsin: Democrat Print Co., 1886.

Appendix D/

Source Books for Identifying Civil War Weapons and Accoutrements*

Albaugh, William A. *Confederate Edged Weapons.* New York: Bonanza Books, 1960.

Albaugh, W. A., Benet, Hugh, Jr., and Simmons, Edward. *Confederate Handguns.* Philadelphia: Riling and Lentz, 1963.

Albaugh, W. A., and Bond, William. *A Photographic Supplement of Confederate Swords.* Washington, D. C.: Published privately by the authors, 1963.

Albaugh, W. A., and Simmons, Edward. *Confederate Arms.* Harrisburg: Stackpole Books, 1957.

Albaugh, W. A., and Steuart, Richard D. *The Original Confederate Colt.* New York: Greenberg, 1953.

Chapel, Charles E. *Gun Collecting.* New York: Coward-McCann, 1947.

————. *The Gun Collector's Handbook of Values.* New York: Coward-McCann, 1970.

Davis, Rollin V. *U. S. Sword Bayonets, 1847–1865.* Harrisburg: Stackpole Books, 1963.

Edwards, W. B. *Civil War Guns.* Harrisburg: Stackpole Books, 1962.

Fuller, Claud E. *Springfield Muzzle Loading Shoulder Arms.* New York: Francis Bannerman Son and S and S Firearms, 1930.

————. *The Breech Loader in the Service.* New Milford, Connecticut: N. Flayderman and Co., 1965.

————. *The Rifled Musket.* Harrisburg: Stackpole Books, 1946.

————. *The Whitney Firearms.* Huntington: Standard Publishing Co., Inc., 1946.

Fuller, Claud E., and Steuart, R. D. *Firearms of the Confederacy.* Huntington, West Virginia: Standard Publications, Inc., 1944.

*Much of this bibliography is from Robert M. Reilly, *United States Military Small Arms, 1816–1865*, pp. 258–59. Reprinted by permission.

Gluckman, Arcadi. *United States Martial Pistols and Revolvers.* Harrisburg: Stackpole Books, 1956.

————. *Identifying Old United States Muskets, Rifles and Carbines.* Buffalo: Otto Ulbrich Co., Inc., 1948.

Hardin, Albert N. *The American Bayonet, 1776–1964.* Philadelphia: Riling and Lentz, 1965.

Hatch, Alden. *Remington Arms in American History.* New York: Published by the author, 1961.

Haven, Charles T. and Belden, Frank A. *A History of the Colt Revolver.* New York: Bonanza Books, 1970.

Hicks, James E. *Notes on United States Ordnance: U. S. Military Firearms, 1776–1946.* LaCanada, California: Published by the author, 1962.

Karr, C. L., and Karr, C. R. *Remington Handguns.* Harrisburg: Stackpole Books, 1956.

Larson, E. Dixon. *Colt Tips.* Union City, Tennessee: Pioneer Press, 1972.

Lewis, B. R. *Small Arms and Ammunition in the United States Service, 1776–1865.* Washington, D. C.: Smithsonian Institution, 1956.

Logan, Herschel C. *Cartridges.* Harrisburg: Stackpole Books, 1959.

Lord, Francis A. *Civil War Collector's Encyclopedia.* Harrisburg: Stackpole Books, 1963.

Lustyik, Andrew F. *Civil War Carbines: From Service to Sentiment.* Aledo, Illinois: Worldwide Gun Report, 1962.

Mitchell, James L. *Colt: A Collection of Letters and Photographs about the Man—the Arms—the Company.* Harrisburg: Stackpole Books, 1959.

Nutter, Waldo E. *Manhattan Firearms.* Harrisburg: Stackpole Books, 1958.

Parsons, John E. *Smith & Wesson Revolvers.* New York: William Morrow and Co., Inc., 1957.

————. *The First Winchester.* New York: William Morrow and Co., Inc., 1955.

Peterson, Harold L. *Notes on Ordnance of the American Civil War, 1861–1865*. Richmond: American Ordnance Association, 1959.

————. *The American Sword, 1775–1945*. New Hope, Pennsylvania: Robert Halter, 1954.

Rankin, Colonel Robert H. *Small Arms of the Sea Service*. New Milford, Connecticut: N. Flayderman, Inc., 1972.

Reilly, Robert M. *United States Military Small Arms, 1816–1865*. Baton Rouge: Eagle Press, 1970.

Riling, Ray. *The Powder Flask Book*. New York: Bonanza Books, 1953.

Serven, James E. *Colt Firearms, 1836–1954*. Santa Ana: Published by the author, 1954.

————. *The Collecting of Guns*. Harrisburg: Stackpole Books, 1964.

Appendix E/
A Selected Bibliography

Amann, William. *Personnel of the Civil War.* Two volumes. New York: Thomas Yoseloff, 1961.

Beers, Henry P. *Guide to the Archives of the Government of the Confederate States of America.* National Archives Publication No. 68–15. Washington: General Services Administration, 1968.

Bibliography of State Participation in the Civil War. Charlottesville, Virginia: Allen Publishing Company, 1961.

Civil War Times Illustrated. Gettysburg, Pa.: Historical Times, Inc., 1962–present.

Colket, Meredith B., Jr., and Bridgers, Frank E. *Guide to Genealogical Records in the National Archives.* Publication No. 64–8, Washington: General Services Administration, 1964.

Cunningham, S. A. *The Confederate Veteran.* Vols. 1–40. Nashville, Tennessee: 1893–1932.

The Confederate Veteran Magazine Index. Vols. I–XL. Dayton, Ohio: The Morningside Bookshop, 1972.

Cullum, George W. *Biographical Register of the Officers and Graduates of the United States Military Academy at West Point, New York, from its Establishment, March 16, 1802, to the Reorganization of 1866–67.* New York: D. Van Nostrand, 1868.

Directory of Historical Societies and Agencies in the United States and Canada. Nashville, Tennessee: American Assn. for State and Local History, 1965.

Dornbusch, Charles E. *Military Bibliography of the Civil War.* Three volumes. New York: The New York Public Library, 1961–72.

Dyer, Frederick H. *A Compendium of the War of the Rebellion.* Des Moines, Iowa: Dyer Publishing Co., 1908. (Reprint) Three Volumes. New York: Thomas Yoseloff, 1959.

Evans, Clement A. *Confederate Military History.* Twelve volumes. Atlanta, Georgia: Confederate Publishing Co., 1899.

Gardner, Alexander. *Gardner's Photographic Sketch Book of the Civil War.* Washington, D. C.: Philip and Solomons, 1865. (Reprint) New York: Dover Press, 1959. (Other reprints)

Hamer, Philip. *A Guide to Archives and Manuscripts in the United States.* New Haven: Yale University Press, 1961.

Hamersly, Thomas H. S. *Complete Regular Army Register of the United States: For 100 Years (1779–1879).* Washington: Thomas H. S. Hamersly, 1880.

Hamersly, Lewis. *The Records of Living Officers of the United States Navy and Marine Corps.* Philadelphia: J. B. Lippincott and Co., 1870.

Heitman, Francis B. *Historical Register and Dictionary of the United States Army, from Its Organization, September 29, 1789, to March 2, 1903.* Washington: Government Printing Office, 1903. (Reprint) Urbana, Illinois: University of Illinois Press, 1965.

List of National Archives Microfilm. Washington: National Archives and Records Service, General Services Administration, 1968.

Military Operations of the Civil War: A Guide-Index to the Official Records of the Union and Confederate Armies, 1861–1865. Washington: National Archives and Records Service, General Services Administration, U. S. Government Printing Office, 1968.

Miller, Francis T. *The Photographic History of the Civil War.* Ten Volumes. New York: Review of Reviews Company, 1911. (Reprint) Five volumes. New York: Thomas Yoseloff, 1957.

Minor, Kate P. *An Author and Subject Index to the Southern Historical Society Papers,* Vols. 1–38. Richmond: Superintendent of Public Printing, 1913. (Reprint) Dayton, Ohio: Morningside Bookshop, 1970.

Munden, Kenneth W., and Beers, Henry P. *Guide to Federal Archives Relating to the Civil War.* National Archives Publication No. 63–1. Washington. General Services Administration, 1962.

The National Union Catalog of Manuscript Collections. Hamden, Connecticut: Shoestring Press, 1961.

Officers in the Confederate States Navy, 1861–65. Naval War Records Office, Government Printing Office, 1898. (Reprint) 1931.

Nevins, Allan; Robertson, James I., Jr.; and Wiley, Bell I. *Civil War Books: A Critical Bibliography.* Two volumes. Baton Rouge: Louisiana State University Press, 1967.

Official Army Register for 1861–1865. Washington: United States Adjutant General's Office, 1861–65.

Official Army Register of the Volunteer Force of the United States Army for the Years 1861–1865. Washington: United States Adjutant General's Office, 1861–65.

United States War Department. *The Official Atlas of the Civil War.* (Reprint) Introduction by Henry Steele Commager. New York: Thomas Yoseloff, 1958.

United States War Department. *Official Records of the Union and Confederate Armies in the War of the Rebellion.* 128 volumes. Washington: United States Government Printing Office, 1901.

United States War Department, *Official Records of the Union and Confederate Navies in the War of the Rebellion.* 31 volumes. Washington: United States Government Printing Office, 1897–1927.

Official Records of the Union and Confederate Navies in the War of the Rebellion: Index. Washington: United States Government Printing Office, 1927. (Reprint) New York: Antiquarian Press, 1961.

Powell, William H. *Officers of the Army and Navy (Regular) Who Served in the Civil War.* Philadelphia: L. R. Hamersly and Co., 1892.

————. *Officers of the Army and Navy (Volunteer) Who Served in the Civil War.* Philadelphia: L. R. Hamersly and Co., 1893.

Smith, Myron J. *American Civil War Navies: A Bibliography.* Metuchen, New Jersey: The Scarecrow Press, 1972.

Symbols of American Libraries. Washington: Library of Congress, 1969.

Tancig, William. *Confederate Military Land Units.* New York: Thomas Yoseloff (A. S. Barnes), 1967.

The Union Army: A History of Military Affairs in the Loyal States, 1861–65. Eight volumes. Madison, Wisconsin: Federal Publishing Co., 1908.

Index

Numbers in italics refer to illustrations

Notes

Notes

Notes

Notes